ALSO BY MICHAEL J. SANDEL

Liberalism and the Limits of Justice (1982; 2nd ed., 1998)

Liberalism and Its Critics (editor) (1984)

Democracy's Discontent: America in Search of a Public Philosophy (1996)

Public Philosophy: Essays on Morality in Politics (2005)

The Case Against Perfection: Ethics in the Age of Genetic Engineering (2007)

Justice: A Reader (editor) (2007)

Justice: What's the Right Thing to Do? (2009)

WHAT MONEY CAN'T BUY

WHAT MONEY CAN'T BUY

The Moral Limits of Markets

MICHAEL J. SANDEL

FARRAR, STRAUS AND GIROUX / NEW YORK

Farrar, Straus and Giroux
18 West 18th Street, New York 10011

Distributed in Canada by D&M Publishers, Inc.
Printed in the United States of America
First edition, 2012

A portion of the introduction originally appeared, in slightly different form, in The Atlantic.

Library of Congress Cataloging-in-Publication Data

Sandel, Michael J.
What money can't buy : the moral limits of markets / Michael J. Sandel. — 1st ed.
p. cm.
Includes bibliographical references and index.
ISBN 978-0-374-20303-0 (alk. paper)
1. Economics—Moral and ethical aspects. 2. Capitalism—Moral and ethical aspects. 3. Wealth—Moral and ethical aspects. 4. Value. I. Title.

HB72 .S255 2012
174—dc23

2011052182

Open Market edition ISBN: 978-0-374-98391-8

Designed by Abby Kagan

www.fsgbooks.com

1 3 5 7 9 10 8 6 4 2

For Kiku, with love

Contents

WHAT MONEY CAN'T BUY

Introduction: Markets and Morals

There are some things money can't buy, but these days, not many. Today, almost everything is up for sale. Here are a few examples:

- *A prison cell upgrade: $82 per night.* In Santa Ana, California, and some other cities, nonviolent offenders can pay for better accommodations—a clean, quiet jail cell, away from the cells for nonpaying prisoners.[1]
- *Access to the car pool lane while driving solo: $8 during rush hour.* Minneapolis and other cities are trying to ease traffic congestion by letting solo drivers pay to drive in car pool lanes, at rates that vary according to traffic.[2]
- *The services of an Indian surrogate mother to carry a pregnancy: $6,250.* Western couples seeking surrogates increasingly outsource the job to India, where the practice is legal and the price is less than one-third the going rate in the United States.[3]
- *The right to immigrate to the United States: $500,000.* Foreigners who invest $500,000 and create at least ten jobs in an area of high unemployment are eligible for a green card that entitles them to permanent residency.[4]

- *The right to shoot an endangered black rhino: $150,000.* South Africa has begun letting ranchers sell hunters the right to kill a limited number of rhinos, to give the ranchers an incentive to raise and protect the endangered species.[5]
- *The cell phone number of your doctor: $1,500 and up per year.* A growing number of "concierge" doctors offer cell phone access and same-day appointments for patients willing to pay annual fees ranging from $1,500 to $25,000.[6]
- *The right to emit a metric ton of carbon into the atmosphere: €13 (about $18).* The European Union runs a carbon emissions market that enables companies to buy and sell the right to pollute.[7]
- *Admission of your child to a prestigious university: ?* Although the price is not posted, officials from some top universities told *The Wall Street Journal* that they accept some less than stellar students whose parents are wealthy and likely to make substantial financial contributions.[8]

Not everyone can afford to buy these things. But today there are lots of new ways to make money. If you need to earn some extra cash, here are some novel possibilities:

- *Rent out space on your forehead (or elsewhere on your body) to display commercial advertising: $777.* Air New Zealand hired thirty people to shave their heads and wear temporary tattoos with the slogan "Need a change? Head down to New Zealand."[9]
- *Serve as a human guinea pig in a drug safety trial for a pharmaceutical company: $7,500.* The pay can be higher or lower, depending on the invasiveness of the procedure used to test the drug's effect, and the discomfort involved.[10]

- *Fight in Somalia or Afghanistan for a private military company: $250 per month to $1,000 per day.* The pay varies according to qualifications, experience, and nationality.[11]
- *Stand in line overnight on Capitol Hill to hold a place for a lobbyist who wants to attend a congressional hearing: $15–$20 per hour.* The lobbyists pay line-standing companies, who hire homeless people and others to queue up.[12]
- *If you are a second grader in an underachieving Dallas school, read a book: $2.* To encourage reading, the schools pay kids for each book they read.[13]
- *If you are obese, lose fourteen pounds in four months: $378.* Companies and health insurers offer financial incentives for weight loss and other kinds of healthy behavior.[14]
- *Buy the life insurance policy of an ailing or elderly person, pay the annual premiums while the person is alive, and then collect the death benefit when he or she dies: potentially, millions (depending on the policy).* This form of betting on the lives of strangers has become a $30 billion industry. The sooner the stranger dies, the more the investor makes.[15]

We live at a time when almost everything can be bought and sold. Over the past three decades, markets—and market values—have come to govern our lives as never before. We did not arrive at this condition through any deliberate choice. It is almost as if it came upon us.

As the cold war ended, markets and market thinking enjoyed unrivaled prestige, understandably so. No other mechanism for organizing the production and distribution of goods had proved as successful at generating affluence and prosperity. And yet, even as growing numbers of countries around the world embraced market mechanisms in the operation of their economies, something else was happening. Market values were coming to play a greater and greater role in social life. Economics was becoming an imperial domain. Today, the logic of buying and selling no longer applies to material goods alone but increasingly governs the whole of life. It is time to ask whether we want to live this way.

THE ERA OF MARKET TRIUMPHALISM

The years leading up to the financial crisis of 2008 were a heady time of market faith and deregulation—an era of market triumphalism. The era began in the early 1980s, when Ronald Reagan and Margaret Thatcher proclaimed their conviction that markets, not government, held the key to prosperity and freedom. And it continued in the 1990s, with the market-friendly liberalism of Bill Clinton and Tony Blair, who moderated but consolidated the faith that markets are the primary means for achieving the public good.

Today, that faith is in doubt. The era of market triumphalism has come to an end. The financial crisis did more than cast doubt on the ability of markets to allocate risk efficiently. It also prompted a widespread sense that markets have become detached from morals and that we need somehow to reconnect them. But it's not obvious what this would mean, or how we should go about it.

Some say the moral failing at the heart of market triumphalism was greed, which led to irresponsible risk taking. The solution, according to this view, is to rein in greed, insist on greater integrity and responsibility among bankers and Wall Street executives, and enact sensible regulations to prevent a similar crisis from happening again.

This is, at best, a partial diagnosis. While it is certainly true that greed played a role in the financial crisis, something bigger is at stake. The most fateful change that unfolded during the past three decades was not an increase in greed. It was the expansion of markets, and of market values, into spheres of life where they don't belong.

To contend with this condition, we need to do more than inveigh against greed; we need to rethink the role that markets should play in our society. We need a public debate about what it means to keep markets in their place. To have this debate, we need to think through the moral limits of markets. We need to ask whether there are some things money should not buy.

The reach of markets, and market-oriented thinking, into aspects of life traditionally governed by nonmarket norms is one of the most significant developments of our time.

Consider the proliferation of for-profit schools, hospitals, and prisons, and the outsourcing of war to private military contractors. (In Iraq and Afghanistan, private contractors actually outnumbered U.S. military troops.[16])

Consider the eclipse of public police forces by private security firms—especially in the United States and Britain, where the number of private guards is more than twice the number of public police officers.[17]

Or consider the pharmaceutical companies' aggressive marketing of prescription drugs to consumers in rich countries. (If you've ever seen the television commercials on the evening news in the United States, you could be forgiven for thinking that the greatest health crisis in the world is not malaria or river blindness or sleeping sickness, but a rampant epidemic of erectile dysfunction.)

Consider too the reach of commercial advertising into public schools; the sale of "naming rights" to parks and civic spaces; the marketing of "designer" eggs and sperm for assisted reproduction; the outsourcing of pregnancy to surrogate mothers in the developing world; the buying and selling, by companies and countries, of the right to pollute; a system of campaign finance that comes close to permitting the buying and selling of elections.

These uses of markets to allocate health, education, public safety, national security, criminal justice, environmental protection, recreation, procreation, and other social goods were for the most part unheard of thirty years ago. Today, we take them largely for granted.

EVERYTHING FOR SALE

Why worry that we are moving toward a society in which everything is up for sale?

For two reasons: one is about inequality; the other is about corruption. Consider inequality. In a society where everything is for sale, life is harder for those of modest means. The more money can buy, the more affluence (or the lack of it) matters.

If the only advantage of affluence were the ability to buy yachts, sports cars, and fancy vacations, inequalities of income and wealth would not matter very much. But as money comes to buy more and more—political influence, good medical care, a home in a safe neighborhood rather than a crime-ridden one, access to elite schools rather than failing ones—the distribution of income and wealth looms larger and larger. Where all good things are bought and sold, having money makes all the difference in the world.

This explains why the last few decades have been especially hard on poor and middle-class families. Not only has the gap between rich and poor widened, the commodification of everything has sharpened the sting of inequality by making money matter more.

The second reason we should hesitate to put everything up for sale is more difficult to describe. It is not about inequality and fairness but about the corrosive tendency of markets. Putting a price on the good things in life can corrupt them. That's because markets don't only allocate goods; they also express and promote certain attitudes toward the goods being exchanged. Paying kids to read books might get them to read more, but also teach them to regard reading as a chore rather than a source of intrinsic satisfaction. Auctioning seats in the freshman class to the highest bidders might raise revenue but also erode the integrity of the college and the value of its diploma. Hiring foreign mercenaries to fight our wars might spare the lives of our citizens but corrupt the meaning of citizenship.

Economists often assume that markets are inert, that they do not affect the goods they exchange. But this is untrue. Markets leave their mark. Sometimes, market values crowd out nonmarket values worth caring about.

Of course, people disagree about what values are worth caring about, and why. So to decide what money should—and should not—be able to buy, we have to decide what values should govern the various domains of social and civic life. How to think this through is the subject of this book.

Here is a preview of the answer I hope to offer: when we decide that certain goods may be bought and sold, we decide, at least implicitly, that it is appropriate to treat them as commodities, as instruments of profit and use. But not all goods are properly valued in this way.[18] The most obvious example is human beings. Slavery was appalling because it treated human beings as commodities, to be bought and sold at auction. Such treatment fails to value human beings in the appropriate way—as persons worthy of dignity and respect, rather than as instruments of gain and objects of use.

Something similar can be said of other cherished goods and practices. We don't allow children to be bought and sold on the market. Even if buyers did not mistreat the children they purchased, a market in children would express and promote the wrong way of valuing them. Children are not properly regarded as consumer goods but as beings worthy of love and care. Or consider the rights and obligations of citizenship. If you are called to jury duty, you may not hire a substitute to take your place. Nor do we allow citizens to sell their votes, even though others might be eager to buy them. Why not? Because we believe that civic duties should not be regarded as private property but should be viewed instead as public responsibilities. To outsource them is to demean them, to value them in the wrong way.

These examples illustrate a broader point: some of the good things in life are corrupted or degraded if turned into commodities. So to decide where the market belongs, and where it should be kept at a distance, we have to decide how to value the goods in question—health, education, family life, nature, art, civic duties, and so on. These are moral and political questions, not merely economic ones. To resolve them, we have to debate, case by case, the moral meaning of these goods and the proper way of valuing them.

This is a debate we didn't have during the era of market triumphalism. As a result, without quite realizing it, without ever deciding to do so, we drifted from *having* a market economy to *being* a market society.

The difference is this: A market economy is a tool—a valuable and effective tool—for organizing productive activity. A market society is a way of life in which market values seep into every aspect of human endeavor. It's a place where social relations are made over in the image of the market.

The great missing debate in contemporary politics is about the role and reach of markets. Do we want a market economy, or a market society? What role should markets play in public life and personal relations? How can we decide which goods should be bought and sold, and which should be governed by nonmarket values? Where should money's writ not run?

These are the questions this book seeks to address. Since they touch on contested visions of the good society and the good life, I can't promise definitive answers. But I hope at least to prompt public discussion of these questions, and to provide a philosophical framework for thinking them through.

RETHINKING THE ROLE OF MARKETS

Even if you agree that we need to grapple with big questions about the morality of markets, you might doubt that our public discourse is up to the task. It's a legitimate worry. Any attempt to rethink the role and reach of markets should begin by acknowledging two daunting obstacles.

One is the persisting power and prestige of market thinking, even in the aftermath of the worst market failure in eighty years. The other is the rancor and emptiness of our public discourse. These two conditions are not entirely unrelated.

The first obstacle is puzzling. At the time, the financial crisis of 2008 was widely seen as a moral verdict on the uncritical embrace of markets that had prevailed, across the political spectrum, for three decades. The near collapse of once-mighty Wall Street financial firms, and the need for a massive bailout at taxpayers' expense, seemed sure to prompt a reconsideration of markets. Even Alan Greenspan, who as chairman of the U.S. Federal Reserve had served as high priest of the market triumphalist faith, admitted to "a state of shocked disbelief" that his confidence in the self-correcting power of free markets turned out to be mistaken.[19] The cover of *The Economist*, the buoyantly pro-market British magazine, showed an economics textbook melting into a puddle, under the headline WHAT WENT WRONG WITH ECONOMICS.[20]

The era of market triumphalism had come to a devastating end. Now, surely, would be a time of moral reckoning, a season of sober second thoughts about the market faith. But things haven't turned out that way.

The spectacular failure of financial markets did little to dampen the faith in markets generally. In fact, the financial crisis discredited government more than the banks. In 2011, surveys found that the American public blamed the federal government more than Wall Street financial institutions for the economic problems facing the country—by a margin of more than two to one.[21]

The financial crisis had pitched the United States and much of the global economy into the worst economic downturn since the Great Depression and left millions of people out of work. Yet it did not prompt a fundamental rethinking of markets. Instead, its most notable political consequence in the United States was the rise of the Tea Party movement, whose hostility to government and embrace of free markets would have made Ronald Reagan blush. In the fall of 2011, the Occupy Wall Street movement brought protests to cities throughout the United States and around the world. These protests targeted big banks and corporate power, and the rising inequality of income and wealth. Despite their different ideological orientations, both the Tea Party and Occupy Wall Street activists gave voice to populist outrage against the bailout.[22]

Notwithstanding these voices of protest, serious debate about the role and reach of markets remains largely absent from our political life. Democrats and Republicans argue, as they long have done, about taxes, spending, and budget deficits, only now with greater partisanship and little ability to inspire or persuade. Disillusion with politics has deepened as citizens grow frustrated with a political system unable to act for the public good, or to address the questions that matter most.

This parlous state of public discourse is the second obstacle to a debate about the moral limits of markets. At a time when political argument consists mainly of shouting matches on cable television, partisan vitriol on talk radio, and ideological food fights on the floor of Congress, it's hard to imagine a reasoned public debate about such controversial moral questions as the right way to value procreation, children, education, health, the environment, citizenship, and other goods. But I believe such a debate is possible, and that it would invigorate our public life.

Some see in our rancorous politics a surfeit of moral conviction: too many people believe too deeply, too stridently, in their own convictions and want to impose them on everyone else. I think this misreads our predicament. The problem with our politics is not too much moral argument but too little. Our politics is overheated because it is mostly vacant, empty of moral and spiritual content. It fails to engage with big questions that people care about.

The moral vacancy of contemporary politics has a number of sources. One is the attempt to banish notions of the good life from public discourse. In hopes of avoiding sectarian strife, we often insist that citizens leave their moral and spiritual convictions behind when they enter the public square. But despite its good intention, the reluctance to admit arguments about the good life into politics prepared the way for market triumphalism and for the continuing hold of market reasoning.

In its own way, market reasoning also empties public life of moral argument. Part of the appeal of markets is that they don't pass judgment on the preferences they satisfy. They don't ask whether some ways of valuing goods are higher, or worthier, than others. If someone is willing to pay for sex or a kidney, and a consenting adult is willing to sell, the only question the economist asks is, "How much?" Markets don't wag fingers. They don't discriminate between admirable preferences and base ones. Each party to a deal decides for himself or herself what value to place on the things being exchanged.

This nonjudgmental stance toward values lies at the heart of market reasoning and explains much of its appeal. But our reluctance to engage in moral and spiritual argument, together with our embrace of markets, has exacted a heavy price: it has drained public discourse of moral and civic energy, and contributed to the technocratic, managerial politics that afflicts many societies today.

A debate about the moral limits of markets would enable us to decide, as a society, where markets serve the public good and where they don't belong. It would also invigorate our politics, by welcoming competing notions of the good life into the public square. For how else could such arguments proceed? If you agree that buying and selling certain goods corrupts or degrades them, then you must believe that some ways of valuing these goods are more appropriate than others. It hardly makes sense to speak of corrupting an activity—parenthood, say, or citizenship—unless you think that some ways of being a parent, or a citizen, are better than others.

Moral judgments such as these lie behind the few limitations on markets we still observe. We don't allow parents to sell their children or citizens to sell their votes. And one of the reasons we don't is, frankly, judgmental: we believe that selling these things values them in the wrong way and cultivates bad attitudes.

Thinking through the moral limits of markets makes these questions unavoidable. It requires that we reason together, in public, about how to value the social goods we prize. It would be folly to expect that a morally more robust public discourse, even at its best, would lead to agreement on every contested question. But it would make for a healthier public life. And it would make us more aware of the price we pay for living in a society where everything is up for sale.

When we think of the morality of markets, we think first of Wall Street banks and their reckless misdeeds, of hedge funds and bailouts and regulatory reform. But the moral and political challenge we face today is more pervasive and more mundane—to rethink the role and reach of markets in our social practices, human relationships, and everyday lives.

1

Jumping the Queue

Nobody likes to wait in line. Sometimes you can pay to jump the queue. It's long been known that, in fancy restaurants, a handsome tip to the maître d' can shorten the wait on a busy night. Such tips are quasi bribes and handled discreetly. No sign in the window announces immediate seating for anyone willing to slip the host a fifty-dollar bill. But in recent years, selling the right to cut in line has come out of the shadows and become a familiar practice.

FAST TRACK

Long lines at airport security checkpoints make air travel an ordeal. But not everyone has to wait in the serpentine queues. Those who buy first-class or business-class tickets can use priority lanes that take them to the front of the line for screening. British Airways calls it Fast Track, a service that also lets high-paying passengers jump the queue at passport and immigration control.[1]

But most people can't afford to fly first-class, so the airlines have begun offering coach passengers the chance to buy line-cutting privileges as an à la carte perk. For an extra $39, United Airlines will sell you priority boarding for your flight from Denver to Boston, along with the right to cut in line at the security checkpoint. In Britain, London's Luton Airport offers an even more affordable fast-track option: wait in the long security line or pay £3 (about $5) and go to the head of the queue.[2]

Critics complain that a fast track through airport security should not be for sale. Security checks, they argue, are a matter of national defense, not an amenity like extra legroom or early boarding privileges; the burden of keeping terrorists off airplanes should be shared equally by all passengers. The airlines reply that everyone is subjected to the same level of screening; only the wait varies by price. As long as everyone receives the same body scan, they maintain, a shorter wait in the security line is a convenience they should be free to sell.[3]

Amusement parks have also started selling the right to jump the queue. Traditionally, visitors may spend hours waiting in line for the most popular rides and attractions. Now, Universal Studios Hollywood and other theme parks offer a way to avoid the wait: for about twice the price of standard admission, they'll sell you a pass that lets you go to the head of the line. Expedited access to the Revenge of the Mummy thrill ride may be morally less freighted than privileged access to an airport security check. Still, some observers lament the practice, seeing it as corrosive of a wholesome civic habit: "Gone are the days when the theme-park queue was the great equalizer," one commentator wrote, "where every vacationing family waited its turn in democratic fashion."[4]

Interestingly, amusement parks often obscure the special privileges they sell. To avoid offending ordinary customers, some parks usher their premium guests through back doors and separate gates; others provide an escort to ease the way of VIP guests as they cut in line. This need for discretion suggests that paid line cutting—even in an amusement park—tugs against a nagging sense that fairness means waiting your turn. But no such reticence appears on Universal's online ticket site, which touts the $149 Front of Line Pass with unmistakable bluntness: "Cut to the FRONT at all rides, shows and attractions!"[5]

If you're put off by queue jumping at amusement parks, you might opt instead for a traditional tourist sight, such as the Empire State Building. For $22 ($16 for children), you can ride the elevator to the eighty-sixth-floor observatory and enjoy a spectacular view of New York City. Unfortunately, the site attracts several million visitors a year, and the wait for the elevator can sometimes take hours. So the Empire State Building now offers a fast track of its own. For $45 per person, you can buy an Express Pass that lets you cut in line—for both the security check and the elevator ride. Shelling out $180 for a family of four may seem a steep price for a fast ride to the top. But as the ticketing website points out, the Express Pass is "a fantastic opportunity" to "make the most of your time in New York—and the Empire State Building—by skipping the lines and going straight to the greatest views."[6]

LEXUS LANES

The fast-track trend can also be seen on freeways across the United States. Increasingly, commuters can buy their way out of bumper-to-bumper traffic and into a fast-moving express lane. It began during the 1980s with car pool lanes. Many states, hoping to reduce traffic congestion and air pollution, created express lanes for commuters willing to share a ride. Solo drivers caught using the car pool lanes faced hefty fines. Some put blow-up dolls in the passenger seat in hopes of fooling the highway patrol. In an episode of the television comedy *Curb Your Enthusiasm*, Larry David comes up with an ingenious way of buying access to the car pool lane: faced with heavy freeway traffic en route to an LA Dodgers baseball game, he hires a prostitute—not to have sex but to ride in his car on the way to the stadium. Sure enough, the quick ride in the car pool lane gets him there in time for the first pitch.[7]

Today, many commuters can do the same—without the need for hired help. For fees of up to $10 during rush hour, solo drivers can buy the right to use car pool lanes. San Diego, Minneapolis, Houston, Denver, Miami, Seattle, and San Francisco are among the cities that now sell the right to a faster commute. The toll typically varies according to the traffic—the heavier the traffic, the higher the fee. (In most places, cars with two or more occupants can still use express lanes for free.) On the Riverside Freeway, east of Los Angeles, rush-hour traffic creeps along at 15–20 miles an hour in the free lanes, while the paying customers in the express lane zip by at 60–65 mph.[8]

Some people object to the idea of selling the right to jump the queue. They argue that the proliferation of fast-track schemes adds to the advantages of affluence and consigns the poor to the back of the line. Opponents of paid express lanes call them "Lexus lanes" and say they are unfair to commuters of modest means. Others disagree. They argue that there is nothing wrong with charging more for faster service. Federal Express charges a premium for overnight delivery. The local dry cleaner charges extra for same-day service.

And yet no one complains that it's unfair for FedEx, or the dry cleaner, to deliver your parcel or launder your shirts ahead of someone else's.

To an economist, long lines for goods and services are wasteful and inefficient, a sign that the price system has failed to align supply and demand. Letting people pay for faster service at airports, at amusement parks, and on highways improves economic efficiency by letting people put a price on their time.

THE LINE-STANDING BUSINESS

Even where you're not allowed to buy your way to the head of the line, you can sometimes hire someone else to queue up on your behalf. Each summer, New York City's Public Theater puts on free outdoor Shakespeare performances in Central Park. Tickets for the evening performances are made available at 1:00 p.m., and the line forms hours in advance. In 2010, when Al Pacino starred as Shylock in *The Merchant of Venice*, demand for tickets was especially intense.

Many New Yorkers were eager to see the play but didn't have time to stand in line. As the *New York Daily News* reported, this predicament gave rise to a cottage industry—people offering to wait in line to secure tickets for those willing to pay for the convenience. The line standers advertised their services on Craigslist and other websites. In exchange for queuing up and enduring the wait, they were able to charge their busy clients as much as $125 per ticket for the free performances.[9]

The theater tried to prevent the paid line standers from plying their trade, claiming "it's not in the spirit of Shakespeare in the Park." The mission of the Public Theater, a publicly subsidized, nonprofit enterprise, is to make great theater accessible to a broad audience drawn from all walks of life. Andrew Cuomo, New York's attorney general at the time, pressured Craigslist to stop running ads for the tickets and line-standing services. "Selling tickets that are meant to be free," he stated, "deprives New Yorkers of enjoying the benefits that this taxpayer-supported institution provides."[10]

Central Park is not the only place where there's money to be made by those who stand and wait. In Washington, D.C., the line-standing business is fast becoming a fixture of government. When congressional committees hold hearings on proposed legislation, they reserve some seats for the press and make others available to the general public on a first-come, first-served basis. Depending on the subject and the size of the room, the lines for the hearings can form a day or more in advance, sometimes in the rain or in the chill of winter. Corporate lobbyists are keen to attend these hearings, in order to chat up lawmakers during breaks and keep track of legislation affecting their industries. But the lobbyists are loath to spend hours in line to assure themselves a seat. Their solution: pay thousands of dollars to professional line-standing companies that hire people to queue up for them.

The line-standing companies recruit retirees, message couriers, and, increasingly, homeless people to brave the elements and hold a place in the queue. The line standers wait outside, then, as the line moves, they proceed inside the halls of the congressional office buildings, queuing up outside the hearing rooms. Shortly before the hearing begins, the well-heeled lobbyists arrive, trade places with their scruffily attired stand-ins, and claim their seats in the hearing room.[11]

The line-standing companies charge the lobbyists $36 to $60 per hour for the queuing service, which means that getting a seat in a committee hearing can cost $1,000 or more. The line standers themselves are paid $10–$20 per hour. *The Washington Post* has editorialized against the practice, calling it "demeaning" to Congress and "contemptuous of the public." Senator Claire McCaskill, a Missouri Democrat, has tried to ban it, without success. "The notion that special interest groups can buy seats at congressional hearings like they would buy tickets to a concert or football game is offensive to me," she said.[12]

The business has recently expanded from Congress to the U.S. Supreme Court. When the Court hears oral arguments in big constitutional cases, it's not easy to get in. But if you're willing to pay, you can hire a line stander to get you a ringside seat in the highest court in the land.[13]

The company LineStanding.com describes itself as "a leader in the Congressional line standing business." When Senator McCaskill proposed legislation to prohibit the practice, Mark Gross, the owner of the company, defended it. He compared line standing to the division of labor on Henry Ford's assembly line: "Each worker on the line was responsible for his/her specific task." Just as lobbyists are good at attending hearings and "analyzing all the testimony," and senators and congressmen are good at "making an informed decision," line standers are good at, well, waiting. "Division of labor makes America a great place to work," Gross claimed. "Linestanding may seem like a strange practice, but it's ultimately an honest job in a free-market economy."[14]

Oliver Gomes, a professional line stander, agrees. He was living in a homeless shelter when he was recruited for the job. CNN interviewed him as he held a place in line for a lobbyist at a hearing on climate change. "Sitting in the halls of Congress made me feel a little better," Gomes told CNN. "It elevated me and made me feel like, well, you know, maybe I do belong here, maybe I can contribute even at that little minute level."[15]

But opportunity for Gomes meant frustration for some environmentalists. When a group of them showed up for the climate change hearing, they couldn't get in. The lobbyists' paid stand-ins had already staked out all the available seats in the hearing room.[16] Of course, it might be argued that if the environmentalists cared enough about attending the hearing, they too could have queued up overnight. Or they could have hired homeless people to do it for them.

TICKET SCALPING DOCTOR APPOINTMENTS

Queuing for pay is not only an American phenomenon. Recently, while visiting China, I learned that the line-standing business has become routine at top hospitals in Beijing. The market reforms of the last two decades have resulted in funding cuts for public hospitals and clinics, especially in rural areas. So patients from the countryside now journey to the major public hospitals in the capital, creating long lines in registration halls. They queue up overnight, sometimes for days, to get an appointment ticket to see a doctor.[17]

The appointment tickets are a bargain—only 14 yuan (about $2). But it isn't easy to get one. Rather than camp out for days and nights in the queue, some patients, desperate for an appointment, buy tickets from scalpers. The scalpers make a business of the yawning gap between supply and demand. They hire people to line up for appointment tickets and then resell the tickets for hundreds of dollars—more than a typical peasant makes in months. Appointments to see leading specialists are especially prized—and hawked by the scalpers as if they were box seats for the World Series. The *Los Angeles*

Times described the ticket-scalping scene outside the registration hall of a Beijing hospital: "Dr. Tang. Dr. Tang. Who wants a ticket for Dr. Tang? Rheumatology and immunology."[18]

There is something distasteful about scalping tickets to see a doctor. For one thing, the system rewards unsavory middlemen rather than those who provide the care. Dr. Tang could well ask why, if a rheumatology appointment is worth $100, most of the money should go to scalpers rather than to him, or his hospital. Economists might agree and advise hospitals to raise their prices. In fact, some Beijing hospitals have added special ticket windows, where the appointments are more expensive and the lines much shorter.[19] This high-priced ticket window is the hospital's version of the no-wait premium pass at amusement parks or the fast-track lane at the airport—a chance to pay to jump the queue.

But regardless of who cashes in on the excess demand, the scalpers or the hospital, the fast track to the rheumatologist raises a more basic question: Should patients be able to jump the queue for medical care simply because they can afford to pay extra?

The scalpers and special ticket windows at Beijing hospitals raise this question vividly. But the same question can be asked of a subtler form of queue jumping increasingly practiced in the U.S.—the rise of "concierge" doctors.

CONCIERGE DOCTORS

Although U.S. hospitals are not thronged with scalpers, medical care often involves a lot of waiting. Doctor appointments have to be scheduled weeks, sometimes months, in advance. When you show up for the appointment, you may have to cool your heels in the waiting room, only to spend a hurried ten or fifteen minutes with the doctor. The reason: Insurance companies don't pay primary care doctors much for routine appointments. So to make a decent living, physicians in general practice have rosters of three thousand patients or more, and often rush through twenty-five to thirty appointments per day.[20]

Many patients and doctors are frustrated with this system, which leaves little time for doctors to get to know their patients or to answer their questions. So a growing number of physicians now offer a more attentive form of care known as "concierge medicine." Like the concierge at a five-star hotel, the concierge physician is at your service around the clock. For annual fees ranging from $1,500 to $25,000, patients are assured of same-day or next-day appointments, no waiting, leisurely consultations, and twenty-four-hour access to the doctor by email and cell phone. And if you need to see a top specialist, your concierge doctor will pave the way.[21]

To provide this attentive service, concierge physicians sharply reduce the number of patients they care for. Physicians who decide to convert their practice into a concierge service send a letter to their existing patients offering a choice: sign up for the new, no-wait service for an annual retainer fee, or find another doctor.[22]

One of the first concierge practices, and one of the priciest, is MD^2 ("MD Squared"), founded in 1996 in Seattle. For a fee of $15,000 per year for an individual ($25,000 for a family), the company promises "absolute, unlimited and exclusive access to your personal physician."[23] Each doctor serves only fifty families. As the company explains on its website, the "availability and level of service we provide absolutely necessitates that we limit our practice to a select few."[24] An article in *Town & Country* magazine reports that the MD^2 waiting room "looks more like the lobby of a Ritz-Carlton than a clinical doctor's office." But few patients even go there. Most are "CEOs and business owners who don't want to lose an hour out of their day to go to the doctor's office and prefer instead to receive care in the privacy of their home or office."[25]

Other concierge practices cater to the upper middle class. MDVIP, a for-profit concierge chain based in Florida, offers same-day appointments and prompt service (answering your call by the second ring) for $1,500 to $1,800 per year, and accepts insurance payments for standard medical procedures. Participating physicians cut their patient rolls to six hundred, enabling them to spend more time with each patient.[26] The company assures patients that "waiting will not be a part of their health care experience." According to *The New York Times*, an MDVIP practice in Boca Raton sets out fruit salad and sponge cake in the waiting room. But since there is little if any waiting, the food often goes untouched.[27]

For concierge doctors and their paying customers, concierge care is everything medicine should be. Doctors can see eight to twelve patients a day, rather than thirty, and still come out ahead financially. Physicians affiliated with MDVIP keep two-thirds of the annual fee (one-third goes to the company), which means a practice with six hundred patients makes $600,000 per year in retainer fees alone, not counting reimbursements from insurance companies. For patients who can afford it, unhurried appointments and round-the-clock access to a doctor are luxuries worth paying for.[28]

The drawback, of course, is that concierge care for a few depends on shunting everyone else onto the crowded rolls of other doctors.[29] It therefore invites the same objection leveled against all fast-track schemes: that it's unfair to those left languishing in the slow lane.

Concierge medicine differs, to be sure, from the special ticket windows and the appointment-scalping system in Beijing. Those who can't afford a concierge doc can generally find decent care elsewhere, while those who can't afford a scalper in Beijing are consigned to days and nights of waiting.

But the two systems have this in common: each enables the affluent to jump the queue for medical care. The queue jumping is more brazen in Beijing than in Boca Raton. There seems a world of difference between the clamor of the crowded registration hall and the calm of the waiting room with the uneaten sponge cake. But that's only because, by the time the concierge patient arrives for his or her appointment, the culling of the queue has already taken place, out of view, by the imposition of the fee.

MARKET REASONING

The stories we've just considered are signs of the times. In airports and amusement parks, in the corridors of Congress and the waiting rooms of doctors, the ethic of the queue—"first come, first-served"—is being displaced by the ethic of the market—"you get what you pay for."

And this shift reflects something bigger—the growing reach of money and markets into spheres of life once governed by nonmarket norms.

Selling the right to cut in line is not the most grievous instance of this trend. But thinking through the rights and wrongs of line standing, ticket scalping, and other forms of queue jumping can help us glimpse the moral force—and moral limits—of market reasoning.

Is there anything wrong with hiring people to stand in line, or with scalping tickets? Most economists say no. They have little sympathy for the ethic of the queue. If I want to hire a homeless person to queue up on my behalf, they ask, why should anyone complain? If

I'd rather sell my ticket than use it, why should I be prevented from doing so?

The case for markets over queues draws on two arguments. One is about respecting individual freedom; the other is about maximizing welfare, or social utility. The first is a libertarian argument. It maintains that people should be free to buy and sell whatever they please, as long as they don't violate anyone's rights. Libertarians oppose laws against ticket scalping for the same reason they oppose laws against prostitution, or the sale of human organs: they believe such laws violate individual liberty, by interfering with the choices made by consenting adults.

The second argument for markets, more familiar among economists, is utilitarian. It says that market exchanges benefit buyers and sellers alike, thereby improving our collective well-being, or social utility. The fact that my line stander and I strike a deal proves that we are both better off as a result. Paying $125 to see the Shakespeare play without having to wait in line must make me better off; otherwise I wouldn't have hired the line stander. And earning $125 by spending hours in a queue must make the line stander better off; otherwise he or she wouldn't have taken the job. We are both better off as a result of our exchange; our utility increases. This is what economists mean when they say that free markets allocate goods efficiently. By allowing people to make mutually advantageous trades, markets allocate goods to those who value them most highly, as measured by their willingness to pay.

My colleague Greg Mankiw, an economist, is the author of one of the most widely used economics textbooks in the United States. He uses the example of ticket scalping to illustrate the virtues of the free market. First, he explains that economic efficiency means allocating goods in a way that maximizes "the economic well-being of everyone in society." He then observes that free markets contribute to this goal by allocating "the supply of goods to the buyers who value them most highly, as measured by their willingness to pay."[30] Consider ticket scalpers: "If an economy is to allocate its scarce resources efficiently, goods must get to those consumers who value them most highly. Ticket scalping is one example of how markets reach efficient outcomes . . . By charging the highest price the market will bear, scalpers help ensure that consumers with the greatest willingness to pay for the tickets actually do get them."[31]

If the free-market argument is correct, ticket scalpers and line-standing companies should not be vilified for violating the integrity of the queue; they should be praised for improving social utility by making underpriced goods available to those most willing to pay for them.

MARKETS VERSUS QUEUES

What, then, is the case for the ethic of the queue? Why try to banish paid line standers and ticket scalpers from Central Park or Capitol Hill? A spokesperson for Shakespeare in the Park offered the following rationale: "They are taking a spot away and a ticket away from someone who wants to be there and is eager to see a production of Shakespeare in the Park. We want people to have that experience for free."[32]

The first part of the argument is flawed. Hired line standers do not reduce the total number of people who see the performance; they only change *who* sees it. It's true, as the spokesperson claims, that the line standers take tickets that would otherwise go to people farther back in the queue who are eager to see the play. But those who wind up with those tickets are also eager to see the play. That's why they shell out $125 to hire a line stander.

What the spokesperson probably meant is that ticket scalping is unfair to those who can't afford the $125. It puts ordinary folks at a disadvantage and makes it harder for them to get tickets. This is a stronger argument. When a line stander or scalper gets a ticket, someone behind him or her in the queue loses out, someone who may be unable to afford the scalper's price.

Free-market advocates might reply as follows: If the theater really wants to fill its seats with people eager to see the play and to maximize the pleasure its performances give, then it should want tickets to go to those who value them most highly. And those are the people who will pay most for a ticket. So the best way to pack the house with an audience that will derive the greatest pleasure from the play is to let the free market operate—either by selling tickets for whatever price the market will bear, or by allowing line standers and scalpers to sell to the highest bidders. Getting tickets to those willing to pay the highest price for them is the best way of determining who most values a Shakespeare performance.

But this argument is unconvincing. Even if your goal is to maximize social utility, free markets may not do so more reliably than queues. The reason is that the willingness to pay for a good does not show who values it most highly. This is because market prices reflect the ability as well as the willingness to pay. Those who most want to see Shakespeare, or the Red Sox, may be unable to afford a ticket. And in some cases, those who pay the most for tickets may not value the experience very highly at all.

I've noticed, for example, that the people sitting in the expensive seats at the ballpark often show up late and leave early. This makes me wonder how much they care about baseball. Their ability to afford seats behind home plate may have more to do with the depth of their pockets than their passion for the game. They certainly don't care as much as some fans, especially young ones, who can't afford box seats but who can tell you the batting average of every player in the starting lineup. Since market prices reflect the ability as well as the willingness to pay, they are imperfect indicators of who most values a particular good.

This is a familiar point, even an obvious one. But it casts doubt on the economist's claim that markets are always better than queues at getting goods to those who value them most highly. In some cases, the willingness to stand in line—for theater tickets or for the ball game—may be a better indicator of who really wants to attend than the willingness to pay.

Defenders of ticket scalping complain that queuing "discriminates in favor of people who have the most free time."[33] That's true, but only in the same sense that markets "discriminate" in favor of people who have the most money. As markets allocate goods based on the ability and willingness to pay, queues allocate goods based on the ability and willingness to wait. And there is no reason to assume that the willingness to pay for a good is a better measure of its value to a person than the willingness to wait.

So the utilitarian case for markets over queues is highly contingent. Sometimes markets do get goods to those who value them most highly; other times, queues may do so. Whether, in any given case, markets or queues do this job better is an empirical question, not a matter that can be resolved in advance by abstract economic reasoning.

MARKETS AND CORRUPTION

But the utilitarian argument for markets over queues is open to a further, more fundamental objection: utilitarian considerations are not the only ones that matter. Certain goods have value in ways that go beyond the utility they give individual buyers and sellers. How a good is allocated may be part of what makes it the kind of good it is.

Think again about the Public Theater's free summer Shakespeare performances. "We want people to have that experience for free," said the spokesperson, explaining the theater's opposition to hired line standers. But why? How would the experience be diminished if tickets were bought and sold? It would be diminished, of course, for those who'd like to see the play but can't afford a ticket. But fairness is not the only thing at stake. Something is lost when free public theater is turned into a market commodity, something beyond the disappointment experienced by those who are priced out of attending.

The Public Theater sees its free outdoor performances as a public festival, a kind of civic celebration. It is, so to speak, a gift the city gives itself. Of course, seating is not unlimited; the entire city cannot attend on any given evening. But the idea is to make Shakespeare freely available to everyone, without regard to the ability to pay. Charging for admission, or allowing scalpers to profit from what is meant to be a gift, is at odds with this end. It changes a public festival into a business, a tool for private gain. It would be as if the city made people pay to watch the fireworks on the Fourth of July.

Similar considerations explain what's wrong with paid line standing on Capitol Hill. One objection is about fairness: it's unfair that wealthy lobbyists can corner the market on congressional hearings, depriving ordinary citizens of the opportunity to attend.

But unequal access is not the only troubling aspect of this practice. Suppose lobbyists were taxed when they hired line-standing companies, and the proceeds were used to make line-standing services affordable for ordinary citizens. The subsidies might take the form, say, of vouchers redeemable for discounted rates at line-standing companies. Such a scheme might ease the unfairness of the present system. But a further objection would remain: turning access to Congress into a product for sale demeans and degrades it.

From an economic point of view, allowing free access to congressional hearings "underprices" the good, giving rise to queues. The line-standing industry remedies this inefficiency by establishing a market price. It allocates seats in the hearing room to those who are willing to pay the most for them. But this values the good of representative government in the wrong way.

We can see this more clearly if we ask why Congress "underprices" admission to its deliberations in the first place. Suppose, striving mightily to reduce the national debt, Congress decided to charge admission to its hearings—$1,000, say, for a front-row seat at the Appropriations Committee. Many people would object, not only on the grounds that the admission fee is unfair to those unable to afford it but also on the grounds that charging the public to attend a congressional hearing is a kind of corruption.

We often associate corruption with ill-gotten gains. But corruption refers to more than bribes and illicit payments. To corrupt a good or a social practice is to degrade it, to treat it according to a lower mode of valuation than is appropriate to it. Charging admission to congressional hearings is a form of corruption in this sense. It treats Congress as if it were a business rather than an institution of representative government.

Cynics might reply that Congress is already a business, in that it routinely sells influence and favors to special interests. So why not acknowledge this openly and charge admission? The answer is that the lobbying, influence peddling, and self-dealing that already afflict Congress are also instances of corruption. They represent the degradation of government in the public interest. Implicit in any charge of corruption is a conception of the purposes and ends an institution (in this case, Congress) properly pursues. The line-standing industry on Capitol Hill, an extension of the lobbying industry, is corrupt in this sense. It is not illegal, and the payments are made openly. But it degrades Congress by treating it as a source of private gain rather than an instrument of the public good.

WHAT'S WRONG WITH TICKET SCALPING?

Why do some instances of paid queue jumping, line standing, and ticket scalping strike us as objectionable, while others do not? The reason is that market values are corrosive of certain goods but appropriate to others. Before we can decide whether a good should be allocated by markets, queues, or in some other way, we have to decide what kind of good it is and how it should be valued.

Figuring this out is not always easy. Consider three examples of "underpriced" goods that have recently given rise to ticket scalping: campsites at Yosemite National Park, open-air masses conducted by Pope Benedict XVI, and live concerts by Bruce Springsteen.

Scalping Campsites at Yosemite

Yosemite National Park, in California, attracts more than four million visitors a year. About nine hundred of its prime campsites can be reserved in advance, at a nominal cost of $20 per night. The reservations can be booked, by telephone or online, beginning at 7:00 a.m. on the fifteenth of each month, up to five months in advance. But it's not easy to get one. Demand is so intense, especially for the summer, that the campsites are fully booked within minutes of becoming available.

In 2011, however, *The Sacramento Bee* reported that ticket scalpers were offering Yosemite campsites for sale on Craigslist for $100 to $150 per night. The National Park Service, which prohibits the resale of reservations, was flooded with complaints about the scalpers and tried to prevent the illicit trade.[34] According to standard market logic, it's not clear why it should: If the National Park Service wants to maximize the welfare society derives from Yosemite, it should want the campsites to be used by those who most value the experience, as measured by their willingness to pay. So rather than try to defeat the scalpers, it should welcome them. Or it should raise the price it charges for campsite reservations to the market-clearing price and eliminate the excess demand.

But the public outrage over the scalping of Yosemite campsites rejects this market logic. The newspaper that broke the story ran an editorial condemning the scalpers under the headline SCALPERS STRIKE YOSEMITE PARK: IS NOTHING SACRED? It saw the scalping as a scam to be prevented, not as a service to social utility. "The wonders of Yosemite belong to all of us," the editorial stated, "not just those who can afford to fork over extra cash to a scalper."[35]

Underlying the hostility to scalping campsites at Yosemite are actually two objections—one about fairness, the other about the proper way of valuing a national park. The first objection worries that scalping is unfair to people of modest means, who can't afford to pay $150 a night for a campsite. The second objection, implied by the editorial's rhetorical question ("Is nothing sacred?") draws on the idea that some things should not be up for sale. According to this idea, national parks are not merely objects of use or sources of social utility. They are places of natural wonder and beauty, worthy of appreciation, even awe. For scalpers to auction access to such places seems a kind of sacrilege.

Papal Masses for Sale

Here is another example of market values colliding with a sacred good: When Pope Benedict XVI made his first visit to the United States, demand for tickets to his stadium masses in New York City and Washington, D.C., far exceeded the supply of seats—even in Yankee Stadium. Free tickets were distributed through Catholic dioceses and local parishes. When the inevitable ticket scalping ensued—one ticket sold online for more than $200—church officials condemned it on the grounds that access to a religious rite should not be bought and sold. "There shouldn't be a market in tickets," a church spokeswoman said. "You can't pay to celebrate a sacrament."[36]

Those who bought tickets from scalpers might disagree. They succeeded in paying to celebrate a sacrament. But the church spokeswoman was trying, I think, to make a different point: although it may be possible to gain admission to a papal mass by buying a ticket from a scalper, the spirit of the sacrament is tainted if the experience is up for sale. Treating religious rituals, or natural wonders, as marketable commodities is a failure of respect. Turning sacred goods into instruments of profit values them in the wrong way.

The Market for Springsteen

But what of an event that is partly a commercial enterprise and partly something else? In 2009, Bruce Springsteen performed two concerts in his home state of New Jersey. He set the highest ticket price at $95, even though he could have charged much more and still filled the arena. This price restraint led to rampant ticket scalping and deprived Springsteen of a lot of money. The Rolling Stones had recently charged $450 for the best seats on their concert tour. Economists who studied ticket prices at an earlier Springsteen concert found that, by charging less than the market price, he had forgone about $4 million that evening.[37]

So why not charge the market price? For Springsteen, keeping ticket prices relatively affordable is a way of keeping faith with his working-class fans. It is also a way of expressing a certain understanding of what his concerts are about. They are moneymaking ventures, to be sure, but only in part. They are also celebratory events whose success depends on the character and composition of the crowd. The performance consists not only in the songs but also in the relationship between the performer and his audience, and the spirit in which they gather.

In a *New Yorker* article on the economics of rock concerts, John Seabrook points out that live concerts are not thoroughgoing commodities, or market goods; to treat them as if they were is to diminish them: "Records are commodities; concerts are social events, and in trying to make a commodity out of the live experience you risk spoiling the experience altogether." He quotes Alan Krueger, an economist who has studied the pricing of Springsteen concerts: "There is still an element of rock concerts that is more like a party than a commodities market." A ticket to a Springsteen concert,

Krueger explained, is not only a market good. It is in some respects a gift. If Springsteen charged as much as the market would bear, he would undermine the gift relation with his fans.[38]

Some may see this as mere public relations, a strategy to forgo some revenue today to preserve goodwill and maximize earnings in the long term. But this is not the only way to make sense of it. Springsteen may believe, and be right to believe, that to treat his live performance as a purely market good would be to demean it, to value it in the wrong way. In this respect at least, he may have something in common with Pope Benedict.

THE ETHIC OF THE QUEUE

We've considered several ways of paying to cut in line: hiring line standers, buying tickets from scalpers, or purchasing line-cutting privileges directly from, say, an airline or an amusement park. Each of these transactions supplants the ethic of the queue (waiting your turn) with the ethic of the market (paying a price for faster service).

Markets and queues—paying and waiting—are two different ways of allocating things, and each is appropriate to different activities. The ethic of the queue, "First come, first served," has an egalitarian appeal. It bids us to ignore privilege, power, and deep pockets—at least for certain purposes. "Wait your turn," we were admonished as children. "Don't cut in line."

The principle seems apt on playgrounds, at bus stops, and when there's a line for the public restroom at a theater or ballpark. We resent people cutting in front of us. If someone with an urgent need asks to jump the queue, most people will oblige. But we'd consider it odd if someone at the back of the line offered us $10 to trade places—or if the management set up express pay toilets alongside the free ones, to accommodate affluent customers (or desperate ones).

But the ethic of the queue does not govern all occasions. If I put my house up for sale, I'm under no obligation to accept the first offer that comes along, simply because it's the first. Selling my house and waiting for a bus are different activities, properly governed by different norms. There's no reason to assume that any single principle—queuing or paying—should determine the allocation of all goods.

Sometimes norms change, and it is unclear which principle should prevail. Think of the recorded message you hear, played over and over, as you wait on hold when calling your bank, HMO, or cable television provider: "Your call will be answered in the order in which it was received." This is the essence of the ethic of the queue. It's as if the company is trying to soothe our impatience with the balm of fairness.

But don't take that recorded message too seriously. Today, some people's calls are answered faster than others. You might call it telephonic queue jumping. Growing numbers of banks, airlines, and credit card companies provide special phone numbers to their best customers or route their calls to elite call centers for prompt attention. Call center technology enables companies to "score" incoming calls and to give faster service to those that come from affluent places. Delta Airlines recently proposed giving frequent flyers a controversial perk: the option of paying $5 extra to speak to a customer service agent in the United States, rather than be routed to a call center in India. Public disapproval led Delta to abandon the idea.[39]

Is there anything wrong with answering the calls of your best (or most promising) customers first? It depends on the kind of good you're selling. Are they calling about an overdraft fee or an appendectomy?

Of course, markets and queues are not the only ways of allocating things. Some goods we distribute by merit, others by need, still others by lottery or chance. Universities typically admit students with the greatest talent and promise, not those who apply first or offer the most money for a place in the freshman class. Hospital emergency rooms treat patients according to the urgency of their condition, not according to the order of their arrival or their willingness to pay extra to be seen first. Jury duty is allocated by lottery; if you are called to serve, you can't hire someone else to take your place.

The tendency of markets to displace queues, and other nonmarket ways of allocating goods, so pervades modern life that we scarcely notice it anymore. It is striking that most of the paid queue-jumping schemes we've considered—at airports and amusement parks, at Shakespeare festivals and congressional hearings, in call centers and doctors' offices, on freeways and in national parks—are recent developments, scarcely imaginable three decades ago. The demise of the queue in these domains may seem a quaint concern. But these are not the only places that markets have invaded.

2

Incentives

CASH FOR STERILIZATION

Each year, hundreds of thousands of babies are born to drug-addicted mothers. Some of these babies are born addicted to drugs, and a great many of them will suffer child abuse or neglect. Barbara Harris, the founder of a North Carolina–based charity called Project Prevention, has a market-based solution: offer drug-addicted women $300 cash if they will undergo sterilization or long-term birth control. More than three thousand women have taken her up on the offer since she launched the program in 1997.[1]

Critics call the project "morally reprehensible," a "bribe for sterilization." They argue that offering drug addicts a financial inducement to give up their reproductive capacity amounts to coercion, especially since the program targets vulnerable women in poor neighborhoods. Rather than help the recipients overcome their addiction, critics complain, the money subsidizes it. As one promotional flyer for the program states, "Don't Let a Pregnancy Ruin Your Drug Habit."[2]

Harris concedes that, more often than not, her clients use the cash to buy more drugs. But she believes this is a small price to pay to prevent children from being born with drug addictions. Some of the women who accept the cash for sterilization have been pregnant a dozen times or more; many already have multiple children in foster care. "What makes a woman's right to procreate more important than the right of a child to have a normal life?" Harris asks. She speaks from experience. She and her husband adopted four children who were born to a crack-addicted woman in Los Angeles. "I'll do anything I have to do to prevent babies from suffering. I don't believe that anybody has the right to force their addiction on another human being."[3]

In 2010, Harris took her incentive scheme to Britain, where the idea of cash for sterilization met strong opposition in the press—an article in the *Telegraph* called it a "creepy proposal"—and from the British Medical Association. Undaunted, Harris has expanded to Kenya, where she pays HIV-positive women $40 to be fitted with intrauterine devices, a form of long-term contraception. In Kenya and South Africa, where Harris plans to go next, health officials and human rights proponents have voiced outrage and opposition.[4]

From the standpoint of market reasoning, it's not clear why the program should provoke outrage. Though some critics say it reminds them of Nazi eugenics, the cash-for-sterilization program is a voluntary arrangement between private parties. The state is not involved, and no one is sterilized against her will. Some argue that drug addicts, desperate for money, are not capable of making a truly voluntary choice when offered easy cash. But if their judgment is that severely impaired, Harris replies, how can they possibly be expected to make sensible decisions about bearing and raising children?[5]

Viewed as a market transaction, the deal produces gains for both parties and increases social utility. The addict gets $300 in exchange for giving up her ability to have children. For their $300, Harris and her organization receive the assurance that the addict will not produce any more drug-addicted babies in the future. According to standard market logic, the exchange is economically efficient. It allocates the good—in this case, control over the addict's reproductive capacity—to the person (Harris) who is willing to pay the most for it and who is therefore presumed to value it most highly.

So why all the fuss? For two reasons, which together shed light on the moral limits of marketing reasoning. Some criticize the cash-for-sterilization deal as coercive; others call it bribery. These are actually different objections. Each points to a different reason to resist the reach of markets into places where they don't belong.

The coercion objection worries that when a drug-addicted woman agrees to be sterilized for money, she is not acting freely. Although no one is holding a gun to her head, the financial inducement may be too tempting to resist. Given her addiction and, in most cases, her poverty, her choice to be sterilized for $300 may not really be free. She may be coerced, in effect, by the necessity of her situation. Of course, people disagree about what inducements, under what circumstances, amount to coercion. So in order to assess the moral status of any market transaction, we have to ask a prior question: Under what conditions do market relations reflect freedom of choice, and under what conditions do they exert a kind of coercion?

The bribery objection is different. It is not about the conditions under which a deal is made but about the nature of the good being bought and sold. Consider a standard case of bribery. If an unscrupulous character bribes a judge or government official to gain an illicit benefit or a favor, the nefarious transaction may be entirely voluntary. Neither party may be coerced, and both may gain. What makes the bribe objectionable is not that it's coercive but that it's corrupt. The corruption consists in buying and selling something (a favorable verdict, say, or political influence) that should not be up for sale.

We often associate corruption with illicit payoffs to public officials. But as we saw in chapter 1, corruption also has a broader meaning: we corrupt a good, an activity, or a social practice whenever we treat it according to a lower norm than is appropriate to it. So, to take an extreme example, having babies in order to sell them for profit is a corruption of parenthood, because it treats children as things to be used rather than beings to be loved. Political corruption can be seen in the same light: when a judge accepts a bribe to render a corrupt verdict, he acts as if his judicial authority were an instrument of personal gain rather than a public trust. He degrades and demeans his office by treating it according to a lower norm than is appropriate to it.

This broader notion of corruption lies behind the charge that the cash-for-sterilization scheme is a form of bribery. Those who call it bribery are suggesting that, whether or not the deal is coercive, it is corrupt. And the reason it is corrupt is that both parties—the buyer (Harris) and the seller (the addict)—value the good being sold (the childbearing capacity of the seller) in the wrong way. Harris treats drug-addicted and HIV-positive women as damaged baby-making machines that can be switched off for a fee. Those who accept her offer acquiesce in this degrading view of themselves. This is the moral force of the bribery charge. Like corrupt judges and public officials, those who get sterilized for money sell something that should not be up for sale. They treat their reproductive capacity as a tool for monetary gain rather than a gift or trust to be exercised according to norms of responsibility and care.

It might be argued, in reply, that the analogy is flawed. A judge who accepts a bribe in exchange for a corrupt verdict sells something that isn't his to sell; the verdict is not his property. But a woman who agrees to be sterilized for pay sells something that belongs to her—namely, her reproductive capacity. Money aside, the woman does no wrong if she chooses to be sterilized (or not to have children); but the judge does wrong to render an unjust verdict even in the absence of a bribe. If a woman has a right to give up her childbearing capacity for reasons of her own, some would argue, she must also have the right to do so for a price.

If we accept this argument, then the cash-for-sterilization deal is not bribery after all. So in order to determine whether a woman's reproductive capacity should be subject to a market transaction, we have to ask what kind of good it is: Should we regard our bodies as possessions that we own and can use and dispose of as we please, or do some uses of our bodies amount to self-degradation? This is a large and controversial question that also arises in debates about prostitution, surrogate motherhood, and the buying and selling of eggs and sperm. Before we can decide whether market relations are appropriate to such domains, we have to figure out what norms should govern our sexual and procreative lives.

THE ECONOMIC APPROACH TO LIFE

Most economists prefer not to deal with moral questions, at least not in their role as economists. They say their job is to explain people's behavior, not judge it. Telling us what norms should govern this or that activity or how we should value this or that good is not, they insist, what they do. The price system allocates goods according to people's preferences; it doesn't assess those preferences as worthy or admirable or appropriate to the circumstance. But despite their protestations, economists increasingly find themselves entangled in moral questions.

This is happening for two reasons: one reflects a change in the world, the other a change in the way economists understand their subject.

In recent decades, markets and market-oriented thinking have reached into spheres of life traditionally governed by nonmarket norms. More and more, we are putting a price on noneconomic goods. Harris's $300 offer is an instance of this trend.

At the same time, economists have been recasting their discipline, making it more abstract and more ambitious. In the past, economists dealt with avowedly economic topics—inflation and unemployment, savings and investment, interest rates and foreign trade. They explained how countries become wealthy and how the price system aligns supply and demand for pork belly futures and other market goods.

Recently, however, many economists have set themselves a more ambitious project. What economics offers, they argue, is not merely a set of insights about the production and consumption of material goods but also a science of human behavior. At the heart of this science is a simple but sweeping idea: In all domains of life, human behavior can be explained by assuming that people decide what to do by weighing the costs and benefits of the options before them, and choosing the one they believe will give them the greatest welfare, or utility.

If this idea is right, then everything has its price. The price may be explicit, as with cars and toasters and pork bellies. Or it may be implicit, as with sex, marriage, children, education, criminal activity, racial discrimination, political participation, environmental protection, even human life. Whether or not we're aware of it, the law of supply and demand governs the provision of all these things.

The most influential statement of this view is offered by Gary Becker, an economist at the University of Chicago, in *The Economic Approach to Human Behavior* (1976). He rejects the old-fashioned notion that economics is "the study of the allocation of material goods." The persistence of the traditional view is due, he speculates, "to a reluctance to submit certain kinds of human behavior to the 'frigid' calculus of economics." Becker seeks to wean us from that reluctance.[6]

According to Becker, people act to maximize their welfare, whatever activity they're engaged in. This assumption, "used relentlessly and unflinchingly, form[s] the heart of the economic approach" to human behavior. The economic approach applies regardless of what goods are at stake. It explains life-and-death decisions and "the choice of a brand of coffee." It applies to choosing a mate and buying a can of paint. Becker continues: "I have come to the position that the economic approach is a comprehensive one that is applicable to all human behavior, be it behavior involving money prices or imputed shadow prices, repeated or infrequent decisions, large or minor decisions, emotional or mechanical ends, rich or poor persons, men or women, adults or children, brilliant or stupid persons, patients or therapists, businessmen or politicians, teachers or students."[7]

Becker does not claim that patients and therapists, businessmen and politicians, teachers and students actually understand their decisions as governed by economic imperatives. But that's only because we're often blind to the wellsprings of our actions. "The economic approach does not assume" that people "are necessarily conscious of their efforts to maximize or can verbalize or otherwise describe in an informative way" the reasons for their behavior. However, those with a keen eye for the price signals implicit in every human situation can see that all our behavior, however remote from material concerns, can be explained and predicted as a rational calculus of costs and benefits.[8]

Becker illustrates his claim with an economic analysis of marriage and divorce:

> According to the economic approach, a person decides to marry when the utility expected from marriage exceeds that expected from remaining single or from additional search for a more suitable mate. Similarly, a married person terminates his (or her) marriage when the utility anticipated from becoming single or marrying someone else exceeds the loss in utility from separation, including losses due to physical separation from one's children, division of joint assets, legal fees, and so forth. Since many persons are looking for mates, a *market* in marriages can be said to exist.[9]

Some think this calculating view takes the romance out of marriage. They argue that love, obligation, and commitment are ideals that can't be reduced to monetary terms. They insist that a good marriage is priceless, something money can't buy.

To Becker, this is a piece of sentimentality that obstructs clear thinking. "With an ingenuity worthy of admiration if put to better use," he writes, those who resist the economic approach explain human behavior as the messy, unpredictable result of "ignorance and irrationality, values and their frequent unexplained shifts, custom and tradition, the compliance somehow induced by social norms." Becker has little patience for this messiness. A single-minded focus on income and price effects, he believes, offers social science a sturdier foundation.[10]

Can all human action be understood in the image of a market? Economists, political scientists, legal scholars, and others continue to debate this question. But what is striking is how potent this image has become—not only in academia but also in everyday life. To a remarkable degree, the last few decades have witnessed the remaking of social relations in the image of market relations. One measure of this transformation is the growing use of monetary incentives to solve social problems.

PAYING KIDS FOR GOOD GRADES

Paying people to be sterilized is one brazen example. Here is another: school districts across the United States now try to improve academic performance by paying children for getting good grades or high scores on standardized tests. The idea that cash incentives can cure what ails our schools looms large in the movement for educational reform.

I attended a very good but excessively competitive public high school in Pacific Palisades, California. I occasionally heard of kids being paid by their parents for every A on their report card. Most of us considered this slightly scandalous. But it never occurred to anyone that the school itself might pay for good grades. I do remember that the Los Angeles Dodgers had a promotion in those years that gave free tickets to high school students who made the honor roll.

We certainly had no objections to this scheme, and my friends and I attended quite a few games. But no one thought of it as an incentive; it was more of a boondoggle.

Things are different now. More and more, financial incentives are seen as a key to educational improvement, especially for students in poorly performing urban schools.

A recent *Time* magazine cover put the question bluntly: "Should Schools Bribe Kids?"[11] Some say it all depends on whether the bribes work.

Roland Fryer, Jr., an economics professor at Harvard, is trying to find out. Fryer, an African American who grew up in tough neighborhoods in Florida and Texas, believes that cash incentives may help motivate kids in inner-city schools. Backed by foundation funding, he has tested his idea in several of the largest school districts in the United States. Beginning in 2007, his project paid out $6.3 million to students in 261 urban schools with predominantly African American and Hispanic populations from low-income families. Different incentive schemes were used in each city.[12]

- In New York City, participating schools paid fourth graders $25 to score well on standardized tests. Seventh graders could earn $50 per test. The average seventh grader made a total of $231.55.[13]
- In Washington, D.C., schools paid middle school students cash rewards for attendance, good behavior, and turning in their homework. Conscientious kids could make up to $100 every two weeks. The average student collected about $40 in the biweekly payoff and a total of $532.85 for the school year.[14]
- In Chicago, they offered ninth graders cash for getting good grades in their courses: $50 for an A, $35 for a B, and $20 for

a C. The top student made a handsome haul of $1,875 for the school year.[15]

- In Dallas, they pay second graders $2 for each book they read. To collect the cash, students have to take a computerized quiz to prove they've read the book.[16]

The cash payments yielded mixed results. In New York City, paying kids for good test scores did nothing to improve their academic performance. The cash for good grades in Chicago led to better attendance but no improvement on standardized tests. In Washington, the payments helped some students (Hispanics, boys, and students with behavior problems) achieve higher reading scores. The cash worked best with the Dallas second graders; the kids who got paid $2 per book wound up with higher reading comprehension scores at the end of the year.[17]

Fryer's project is one of many recent attempts to pay kids to do better in school. Another such program offers cash for good scores on Advanced Placement exams. AP courses expose high school students to challenging college-level material in math, history, science, English, and other subjects. In 1996, Texas launched the Advanced Placement Incentive Program, which pays students from $100 to $500 (depending on the school) for earning a passing grade (a score of 3 or higher) on AP exams. Their teachers are also rewarded, with $100 to $500 for each student who passes the exam, plus additional salary bonuses. The incentive program, which now operates in sixty Texas high schools, seeks to improve the college readiness of minority and low-income students. A dozen states now offer financial incentives to students and teachers for success on AP tests.[18]

Some incentive programs target teachers rather than students. Although teachers' unions have been wary of pay-for-performance proposals, the idea of paying teachers for the academic achievement of their students is popular among voters, politicians, and some educational reformers. Since 2005, school districts in Denver; New York City; Washington, D.C.; Guilford County, North Carolina; and Houston have implemented cash incentive schemes for teachers. In 2006, Congress established the Teacher Incentive Fund to provide pay-for-performance grants for teachers in low-achieving schools. The Obama administration increased funding for the program. Recently, a privately funded incentive project in Nashville offered middle school math teachers cash bonuses of up to $15,000 for improving the test scores of their students.[19]

The bonuses in Nashville, sizable though they were, had virtually no impact on students' math performance. But the Advanced Placement incentive programs in Texas and elsewhere have had a positive effect. More students, including students from low-income and minority backgrounds, have been encouraged to take AP courses. And many are passing the standardized exams that qualify them for college credit. This is very good news. But it does not bear out the standard economic view about financial incentives: the more you pay, the harder students will work, and the better the outcome. The story is more complicated.

The AP incentive programs that have succeeded offer more than cash to students and teachers; they transform the culture of schools and the attitudes of students toward academic achievement. Such programs provide special training for teachers, laboratory equipment, and organized tutoring sessions after school and on Saturdays. One tough urban school in Worcester, Massachusetts, made AP classes available to all students, rather than to a preselected elite, and recruited students with posters featuring rap stars, "making it cool for boys with low-slung jeans who idolize rappers like Lil

Wayne to take the hardest classes." The $100 incentive for passing the AP test at the end of the year was a motivator, it seems, more for its expressive effect than for the money itself. "There's something cool about the money," one successful student told *The New York Times.* "It's a great extra." The twice-weekly after-school tutoring sessions and eighteen hours of Saturday classes provided by the program also helped.[20]

When an economist looked closely at the Advanced Placement incentive program in low-income Texas schools, he found something interesting: the program succeeded in boosting academic achievement but not in a way that the standard "price effect" would predict (the more you pay, the better the grades). Although some schools paid $100 for a passing grade on the AP test, and others paid as much as $500, the results were no better in schools that offered the higher amounts. Students and teachers were "not simply behaving like revenue maximizers," wrote C. Kirabo Jackson, the author of the study.[21]

So what was going on? The money had an expressive effect—making academic achievement "cool." That's why the amount was not decisive. Although only AP courses in English, math, and science qualified for the cash incentives at most schools, the program also led to higher enrollment in other AP courses, such as history and social studies. The Advanced Placement incentive programs have succeeded not by bribing students to achieve but by changing attitudes toward achievement and the culture of schools.[22]

HEALTH BRIBES

Health care is another area where cash incentives are in vogue. Increasingly, doctors, insurance companies, and employers are paying people to be healthy—to take their medications, to quit smoking, to lose weight. You might think that avoiding disease or life-threatening ailments would be motivation enough. But, surprisingly, that's often not the case. One-third to one-half of patients fail to take their medications as prescribed. When their conditions worsen, the overall result is billions of dollars a year in additional health costs. So doctors and insurers are offering cash incentives to motivate patients to take their meds.[23]

In Philadelphia, patients prescribed warfarin, an anti–blood clot medication, can win cash rewards ranging from $10 to $100 for taking the drug. (A computerized pillbox records whether they take the drug and tells them whether they won that day.) Participants in the incentive scheme make an average of $90 a month for adhering to their prescriptions. In Britain, some patients with bipolar disorder or schizophrenia are paid £15 (about $22) to show up for their monthly injection of antipsychotic drugs. Teenage girls are offered £45 (about $68) in shopping vouchers to receive vaccinations that protect against a sexually transmitted virus that can cause cervical cancer.[24]

Smoking imposes big costs on companies that provide health insurance to their workers. So in 2009, General Electric began paying some of its employees to quit smoking—$750 if they could quit for as long as a year. The results were so promising that GE has extended the offer to all its U.S. employees. The Safeway grocery store chain offers lower health-insurance premiums to workers who don't smoke and who keep their weight, blood pressure, and cholesterol under control. A growing number of companies use some combination of carrots and sticks to motivate employees to improve their health. Eighty percent of big U.S. companies now offer financial incentives for those who participate in wellness programs. And almost half penalize workers for unhealthy habits, typically by charging them more for health insurance.[25]

Weight loss is the most alluring if intractable target of cash incentive experiments. The NBC reality show *The Biggest Loser* dramatizes the current craze of paying people to slim down. It offers $250,000 to the contestant who achieves the biggest proportional weight loss during the season.[26]

Doctors, researchers, and employers have tried offering more modest incentives. In one U.S. study, a reward of a few hundred dollars motivated obese participants to shed about fourteen pounds in four months. (Unfortunately, the weight losses proved temporary.) In Britain, where the National Health Service spends 5 percent of its budget treating obesity-related diseases, the NHS tried paying overweight people up to £425 (about $612) to lose weight and keep it off for two years. The scheme is called Pounds for Pounds.[27]

Two questions can be asked about paying people for healthy behavior: Does it work? and, Is it objectionable?

From an economic point of view, the case for paying people for good health is a simple matter of costs and benefits. The only real question is whether incentive schemes work. If money motivates people to take their meds, quit smoking, or join a gym, thus reducing the need for expensive care later, why object?

And yet many do object. The use of cash incentives to promote healthy behavior generates fierce moral controversy. One objection is about fairness, the other about bribery. The fairness objection is voiced, in different ways, on both sides of the political spectrum. Some conservatives argue that overweight people should slim down on their own; paying them to do so (especially with taxpayer funds) unfairly rewards slothful behavior. These critics see cash incentives as a "reward for indulgence rather than a form of treatment." Underlying this objection is the idea that "we can all control our own weight," so it's unfair to pay those who have failed to do so on their own—especially if the payments come, as they sometimes do in Britain, from the National Health Service. "Paying someone to ditch bad habits is the ultimate in nanny state mentality, absolving them of any responsibility for their health."[28]

Some liberals voice the opposite worry: that financial rewards for good health (and penalties for bad health) can unfairly disadvantage people for medical conditions beyond their control. Allowing companies or health insurers to discriminate between the healthy and the unhealthy in setting insurance premiums is unfair to those who, through no fault of their own, are less healthy and so at greater risk. It is one thing to give everyone a discount for joining a gym, but something else to set insurance rates based on health outcomes that many people can't control.[29]

The bribery objection is more elusive. The press commonly calls health incentives bribes. But are they? In the cash for sterilization scheme, the bribery is clear. Women are paid to relinquish their reproductive capacity not for their own good but for the sake of an external end—preventing more drug-addicted babies. They are being paid to act, in many cases at least, against their interest.

But the same can't be said of cash incentives to help people stop smoking or lose weight. Whatever external ends may be served (such as reducing health costs for companies or a national health service), the money encourages behavior that promotes the health of the recipient. So how is it a bribe?[30] Or, to ask a slightly different question, why does the charge of bribery seem to fit, even though healthy behavior is in the interest of the person being bribed?

It fits, I think, because we suspect that the monetary motive crowds out other, better motives. Here's how: Good health is not only about achieving the right cholesterol level and body mass index. It is also about developing the right attitude to our physical well-being and treating our bodies with care and respect. Paying people to take their meds does little to develop such attitudes and may even undermine them.

This is because bribes are manipulative. They bypass persuasion and substitute an external reason for an intrinsic one. "You don't care enough about your own well-being to quit smoking or lose weight? Then do it because I'll pay you $750."

Health bribes trick us into doing something we should be doing anyhow. They induce us to do the right thing for the wrong reason. Sometimes, it helps to be tricked. It isn't easy to quit smoking or lose weight on our own. But eventually, we should rise above manipulation. Otherwise, the bribe may become habit forming.

If health bribes work, worries about corrupting good attitudes toward health may seem hopelessly high-minded. If cash can cure us of obesity, why cavil about manipulation? One answer is that a proper concern for our physical well-being is a part of self-respect. Another answer is more practical: absent the attitudes that sustain good health, the pounds may return when the incentives end.

This seems to have happened in the paid weight-loss schemes that have been studied so far. Cash to quit smoking has shown a glimmer of hope. But even the most encouraging study found that more than 90 percent of smokers who were paid for kicking the habit were back to smoking six months after the incentives ended. In general, cash incentives seem to work better at getting people to show up for a specific event—a doctor's appointment or an injection—than at changing long-term habits and behaviors.[31]

Paying people to be healthy can backfire, by failing to cultivate the values that sustain good health. If this is true, the economist's question ("Do cash incentives work?") and the moralist's question ("Are they objectionable?") are more closely connected than first appears. Whether an incentive "works" depends on the goal. And the goal, properly conceived, may include values and attitudes that cash incentives undermine.

PERVERSE INCENTIVES

A friend of mine used to pay his young children $1 each time they wrote a thank-you note. (I could usually tell by reading the notes that they were written under duress.) This policy may or may not work in the long run. It might turn out that, by writing enough thank-you notes, the children will eventually learn the real point of them and continue to express gratitude for gifts, even when they are no longer paid to do so. It's also possible that they will absorb the wrong lesson, and regard thank-you notes as piecework, a burden to be performed for pay. In this case, the habit won't take, and they will stop writing such notes once they are no longer paid. Worse, the bribes may corrupt their moral education and make it harder for them to learn the virtue of gratitude. Even if it increases production in the short run, the bribe for thank-you notes will have failed, by inculcating the wrong way of valuing the good in question.

A similar question arises in the case of cash for good grades: Why not pay a child for getting good grades or for reading a book? The goal is to motivate the child to study or to read. The payment is an incentive to promote that end. Economics teaches that people respond to incentives. And while some children may be motivated to read books for the love of learning, others may not. So why not use money as a further incentive?

It may turn out—as economic reasoning suggests—that two incentives work better than one. But it could also turn out that the monetary incentive undermines the intrinsic one, leading to less reading rather than more. Or to more reading in the short run but for the wrong reason.

In this scenario, the market is an instrument, but not an innocent one. What begins as a market mechanism becomes a market norm. The obvious worry is that the payment may habituate children to think of reading books as a way of making money, and so erode, or crowd out, or corrupt the love of reading for its own sake.

The use of cash incentives to get people to lose weight or read books or be sterilized reflects the logic of the economic approach to life, but also extends it. When Gary Becker wrote, in the mid-1970s, that everything we do can be explained by assuming that we calculate costs and benefits, he referred to "shadow prices"—the imaginary prices said to be implicit in the alternatives we face and the choices we make. So, for example, when a person decides to stay married rather than get a divorce, no prices are posted; rather, the person considers the implicit price of a breakup—the financial price and the emotional price—and decides the benefits aren't worth it.

But the incentive schemes that abound today go further. By putting an actual, explicit price on activities far removed from material pursuits, they take Becker's shadow prices out of the shadows and make them real. They enact his suggestion that all human relations are, ultimately, market relations.

Becker himself made a striking proposal along these lines, a market solution to the contentious debate over immigration policy: the United States should scrap its complex system of quotas, point systems, family preferences, and queues and simply sell the right to immigrate. Given the demand, Becker suggests setting the price of admission at $50,000, or perhaps higher.[32]

Immigrants willing to pay a large entrance fee, Becker reasons, would automatically have desirable characteristics. They would likely be young, skilled, ambitious, hardworking, and unlikely to make use of welfare or unemployment benefits. When Becker first proposed selling the right to immigrate in 1987, many considered the notion far-fetched. But to those steeped in economic thinking, it was a sensible, even obvious way of bringing market reasoning to bear on an otherwise thorny question: How should we decide which immigrants to admit?

Julian L. Simon, another economist, proposed a similar plan at about the same time. He suggested setting a yearly quota of immigrants to be admitted, and auctioning admission to the highest bidders until the quota was filled. Selling the right to immigrate is fair, Simon argued, "because it discriminates according to the standard of a market-oriented society: ability and willingness to pay." To address the objection that his plan would allow only the wealthy to enter, Simon suggested allowing the winning bidders to borrow some of their entry fee from the government and pay it back later with their income tax. If they were unable to repay, he observed, they could always be deported.[33]

The idea of selling the right to immigrate was offensive to some. But in an age of rising market faith, the gist of the Becker-Simon proposal soon found its way into law. In 1990, Congress provided that foreigners who invested $500,000 in the United States could immigrate, with their families, for two years, after which they could receive a permanent green card if the investment created at least ten jobs. The cash-for-green-card plan was the ultimate queue-jumping scheme, a fast track to citizenship. In 2011, two senators proposed a bill offering a similar cash incentive to boost the high-end housing market, which was still weak in the aftermath of the financial crisis. Any foreigner who bought a $500,000 house would receive a visa allowing the buyer, spouse, and minor children to live in the United States as long as they owned the property. A headline in *The Wall Street Journal* summed up the deal: BUY HOUSE, GET A VISA.[34]

Becker even proposed charging admission to refugees fleeing persecution. The free market, he claimed, would make it easy to decide which refugees to accept—those sufficiently motivated to pay the price: "For obvious reasons, political refugees and those persecuted in their own countries would be willing to pay a sizeable fee to gain admission to a free nation. So a fee system would automatically avoid time-consuming hearings about whether they are really in physical danger if they were forced to return home."[35]

Asking a refugee fleeing persecution to hand over $50,000 may strike you as callous, yet another instance of the economist's failure to distinguish between the willingness and the ability to pay. So consider another market proposal to solve the refugee problem, one that doesn't make the refugees pay out of pocket. Peter Schuck, a law professor, proposed the following:

Let an international body assign each country a yearly refugee quota, based on national wealth. Then let nations buy and sell these obligations among themselves. So, for example, if Japan is allocated twenty thousand refugees per year but doesn't want to take them, it could pay Russia, or Uganda, to take them in. According to standard market logic, everyone benefits. Russia or Uganda gains a new source of national income, Japan meets its refugee obligations by outsourcing them, and more refugees are rescued than would otherwise find asylum.[36]

There is something distasteful about a market in refugees, even if it leads to more refugees finding asylum. But what exactly is objectionable about it? It has something to do with the fact that a market in refugees changes our view of who refugees are and how they should be treated. It encourages the participants—the buyers, the sellers, and also those whose asylum is being haggled over—to think of refugees as burdens to be unloaded or as revenue sources, rather than as human beings in peril.

One might acknowledge the degrading effect of a market in refugees and still conclude that the scheme does more good than harm. But what the example illustrates is that markets are not mere mechanisms. They embody certain norms. They presuppose—and promote—certain ways of valuing the goods being exchanged.

Economists often assume that markets do not touch or taint the goods they regulate. But this is untrue. Markets leave their mark on social norms. Often, market incentives erode or crowd out nonmarket incentives.

A study of some child-care centers in Israel shows how this can happen. The centers faced a familiar problem: parents sometimes came late to pick up their children. A teacher had to stay with the children until the tardy parents arrived. To solve this problem, the centers imposed a fine for late pickups. What do you suppose happened? Late pickups actually increased.[37]

Now if you assume that people respond to incentives, this is a puzzling result. You would expect the fine to reduce, not increase, the incidence of late pickups. So what happened? Introducing the monetary payment changed the norms. Before, parents who came late felt guilty; they were imposing an inconvenience on the teachers. Now parents considered a late pickup as a service for which they were willing to pay. They treated the fine as if it were a fee. Rather than imposing on the teacher, they were simply paying him or her to work longer.

FINES VERSUS FEES

What is the difference between a fine and a fee? It's worth pondering the distinction. Fines register moral disapproval, whereas fees are simply prices that imply no moral judgment. When we impose a fine for littering, we're saying that littering is wrong. Tossing a beer can into the Grand Canyon not only imposes cleanup costs. It reflects a bad attitude that we as a society want to discourage. Suppose the fine is $100, and a wealthy hiker decides it's worth the convenience of not having to carry his empties out of the park. He treats the fine as a fee and tosses his beer cans into the Grand Canyon. Even though he pays up, we consider that he's done something wrong. By treating the Grand Canyon as an expensive Dumpster, he has failed to appreciate it in an appropriate way.

Or consider parking spaces reserved for use by the physically disabled. Suppose a busy able-bodied contractor wants to park near his building site. For the convenience of parking his car in a place reserved for the disabled, he is willing to pay the rather large fine; he considers it a cost of doing business. Although he pays the fine, don't we consider that he's doing something wrong? He treats the fine as if it were simply an expensive parking lot fee. But this misses its moral significance. In treating the fine as a fee, he fails to respect the needs of the physically disabled and the desire of the community to accommodate them by setting aside certain parking spaces.

The $217,000 Speeding Ticket

When people treat fines as fees, they flout the norms that fines express. Often, society strikes back. Some affluent drivers consider speeding tickets the price they pay for driving as fast as they please. In Finland, the law leans hard against that way of thinking (and driving) by basing fines on the income of the offender. In 2003, Jussi Salonoja, the twenty-seven-year-old heir to a sausage business, was fined €170,000 (about $217,000 at the time) for driving 80 kilometers per hour (50 mph) in a 40 km/h (25 mph) zone. Salonoja, one of the richest men in Finland, had an income of €7 million per year. The previous record for the most expensive speeding ticket was held by Anssi Vanjoki, an executive of Nokia, the mobile phone company. In 2002, he was fined €116,000 for speeding through Helsinki on his Harley-Davidson. A judge reduced the fine when Vanjoki showed that his income had dropped, due to a downturn in Nokia's profits.[38]

What makes the Finnish speeding tickets fines rather than fees is not only the fact that they vary with income. It's the moral opprobrium that lies behind them—the judgment that violating the speed limit is wrong. Progressive income taxes also vary with income, and yet they are not fines; their purpose is to raise revenue, not to penalize income-producing activity. Finland's $217,000 speeding ticket shows that society not only wants to cover the costs of risky behavior; it also wants the punishment to fit the crime—and the bank balance of the perpetrator.

Notwithstanding the cavalier attitude of some fast-driving rich folk toward speed limits, the distinction between a fine and a fee is not easily effaced. In most places, being pulled over and issued a speeding ticket still carries a stigma. No one thinks the officer is simply collecting a toll, or presenting the offender with a bill for the convenience of a faster commute. I recently ran across a bizarre proposal that makes this clear, by showing what a speeding fee rather than fine would actually look like.

In 2010, Eugene "Gino" DiSimone, an independent candidate for governor of Nevada, proposed an unusual way to raise money for the state budget: allow people to pay $25 per day to exceed the posted speed limit and drive ninety miles per hour on designated roads in Nevada. If you wanted the option of speeding from time to time, you would buy a transponder and dial into your account by cell phone whenever you needed to get somewhere fast. The $25 would be charged to your credit card, and you would be free to speed for the next twenty-four hours without being pulled over. If an officer with a radar gun detected you barreling down the highway, the transponder would signal that you were a paying customer, and no ticket would be issued. DiSimone estimated that his proposal would raise at least $1.3 billion a year for the state, without raising taxes. Despite the tempting windfall to the state budget, the Nevada Highway Patrol said the plan would imperil public safety, and the candidate went down to defeat.[39]

Subway Cheats and Video Rentals

In practice, the distinction between a fine and a fee can be unstable, even contestable. Consider this: If you ride the Paris Métro without paying the $2 fare, you can be fined up to $60. The fine is a penalty for cheating the system by evading the fare. Recently, however, a group of habitual fare dodgers came up with a clever way of converting the fine into a fee, and a modest one at that. They formed an insurance fund that will pay their fine if they get caught. Each member pays in about $8.50 a month to the fund (called a *mutuelle des fraudeurs*), far less than the $74 it costs to buy a legitimate monthly pass.

The members of the *mutuelle* movement say they are motivated not by money but by an ideological commitment to free public transportation. "It's a way to resist together," a leader of the group told the *Los Angeles Times*. "There are things in France which are supposed to be free—schools, health. So why not transportation?" Although the *fraudeurs* are unlikely to prevail, their novel scheme converts a penalty for cheating into a monthly insurance premium, a price they are willing to pay to resist the system.[40]

To decide whether a fine or a fee is appropriate, we have to figure out the purpose of the social institution in question and the norms that should govern it. The answer will vary depending on whether we're talking about showing up late at the day-care center, jumping the turnstile in the Paris subway, or . . . returning an overdue DVD to the local video store.

In the early days of video stores, they treated late fees as fines. If I returned a video late, the person behind the counter had a certain attitude. It was as if I'd done something morally wrong, keeping the movie an extra three days. I thought this attitude was misplaced. A commercial video store is not a public library, after all. Libraries impose fines for overdue books, not fees. That's because their purpose is to organize the free sharing of books within a community. So it's right that I feel guilty when I slink back with an overdue library book.

But a video store is a business. Its purpose is to make money by renting videos. So if I keep the movie longer and pay for the extra days, I should be regarded as a better customer, not a worse one. Or so I thought. Gradually, this norm has shifted. Video stores now seem to treat overdue charges as fees rather than fines.

China's One-Child Policy

Often, the moral stakes are higher. Consider this controversy over the sometimes blurry line between a fine and a fee: in China, the fine for violating the government's one-child policy is increasingly regarded by the affluent as a price for an extra child. The policy, put in place more than three decades ago to reduce China's population growth, limits most couples in urban areas to one child. (Rural families are allowed a second child if the first one is a girl.) The fine varies from region to region but reaches 200,000 yuan (about $31,000) in major cities—a staggering figure for the average worker but easily affordable for wealthy entrepreneurs, sports stars, and celebrities. One account from a Chinese news agency tells of a pregnant woman and her husband in Guangzhou who "strutted in" to their local birth control office, threw the money on the desk, and said, "Here is 200,000 yuan. We need to take care of our future baby. Please do not come to disturb us."[41]

Family-planning officials have sought to reassert the punitive aspect of the sanction by increasing fines for affluent offenders, denouncing celebrities who violate the policy and banning them from appearing on television, and preventing business executives with extra kids from receiving government contracts. "The fine is a piece of cake for the rich," explained Zhai Zhenwu, a professor of sociology at Renmin University. "The government had to hit them harder where it really hurt, at their fame, reputation, and standing in society."[42]

The authorities regard the fine as a penalty and want to preserve the stigma associated with it. They don't want it to devolve into a fee. This is not mainly because they're worried about affluent parents having too many children; the number of wealthy offenders is relatively small. What's at stake is the norm underlying the policy. If the fine were merely a fee, the state would find itself in the awkward business of selling the right to have extra children to those able and willing to pay for it.

Tradable Procreation Permits

Oddly enough, some Western economists have called for a market-based approach to population control strikingly similar to the fee-based system the Chinese officials are trying to avoid. These economists have urged countries that need to limit their population to issue tradable procreation permits. In 1964, the economist Kenneth Boulding proposed a system of marketable procreation licenses as a way of dealing with overpopulation. Each woman would be issued a certificate (or two, depending on the policy) entitling her to have a child. She would be free to use the certificate or sell it at the going rate. Boulding imagined a market in which people eager to have children would purchase certificates from (as he indelicately put it) "the poor, the nuns, the maiden aunts, and so on."[43]

The plan would be less coercive than a system of fixed quotas, as in a one-child policy. It would also be economically more efficient, since it would get the goods (in this case, children) to the consumers most willing to pay for them. Recently, two Belgian economists revived Boulding's proposal. They pointed out that, since the rich would likely buy procreation licenses from the poor, the scheme would have the further advantage of reducing inequality by giving the poor a new source of income.[44]

Some people oppose all restrictions on procreation, while others believe that reproductive rights can legitimately be restricted to avoid overpopulation. Set aside for the moment that disagreement of principle and imagine a society that was determined to implement mandatory population control. Which policy would you find less objectionable: a fixed quota system that limits each couple to one child and fines those who exceed the limit, or a market-based system that issues each couple a tradable procreation voucher entitling the bearer to have one child?

From the standpoint of economic reasoning, the second policy is clearly preferable. The freedom to choose whether to use the voucher or sell it makes some people better off and no one worse off. Those who buy or sell vouchers gain (by making mutually advantageous trades) and those who don't enter the market are no worse off than they would be under the fixed quota system; they can still have one child.

And yet there is something troubling about a system in which people buy and sell the right to have kids. Part of what's troubling is the unfairness of such a system under conditions of inequality. We hesitate to make children a luxury good, affordable by the rich but not the poor. If having children is a central aspect of human flourishing, then it's unfair to condition access to this good on the ability to pay.

Beyond the fairness objection is the question of bribery. At the heart of the market transaction is a morally disquieting activity: parents who want an extra child must induce or entice other prospective parents to sell off their right to have a child. Morally, it's not much different from buying a couple's only child after it has been born.

Economists might argue that a market in children, or in the right to have them, has the virtue of efficiency: it allocates kids to those who value them most highly, as measured by the ability to pay. But trafficking in the right to procreate promotes a mercenary attitude toward children that corrupts parenthood. Central to the norm of parental love is the idea that one's children are inalienable; it is unthinkable to put them up for sale. So to buy a child, or the right to have one, from another prospective parent is to cast a shadow over parenthood as such. Wouldn't the experience of loving your children be tainted if you acquired some of them by bribing other couples to remain childless? Might you be tempted, at least, to hide this fact from your children? If so, there is reason to conclude that, whatever its advantages, a market in procreation permits would corrupt parenthood in ways that a fixed quota, however odious, would not.

Tradable Pollution Permits

The distinction between a fine and a fee is also relevant to the debate over how to reduce greenhouse gases and carbon emissions. Should government set limits on emissions and fine companies that exceed them? Or should government create tradable pollution permits? The second approach says in effect that emitting pollution is not like littering but simply a cost of doing business. But is that right? Or should some moral stigma attach to companies that spew excessive pollution into the air? To decide this question, we need not only to calculate costs and benefits; we have to decide what attitudes toward the environment we want to promote.

At the Kyoto conference on global warming (1997), the United States insisted that any mandatory worldwide emissions standards would have to include a trading scheme, allowing countries to buy and sell the right to pollute. So, for example, the United States could fulfill its obligations under the Kyoto Protocol by either reducing its own greenhouse gas emissions or paying to reduce emissions someplace else. Rather than tax gas-guzzling Hummers at home, it could pay to restore an Amazonian rain forest or modernize an old coal-burning factory in a developing country.

At the time, I wrote an op-ed in *The New York Times* arguing against the trading scheme. I worried that letting countries buy the right to pollute would be like letting people pay to litter. We should try to strengthen, not weaken, the moral stigma attached to despoiling the environment. I also worried that, if rich countries could buy their way out of the duty to reduce their own emissions, we would undermine the sense of shared sacrifice necessary to future global cooperation on the environment.[45]

The *Times* was flooded with scathing letters—mostly from economists, some of them my Harvard colleagues. I failed to understand the virtue of markets, they suggested, or the efficiencies of trade, or the elementary principles of economic rationality.[46] Amid the torrent of criticism, I did receive a sympathetic email from my old college economics professor. He understood the point I was trying to make, he wrote. But he also asked a small favor: Would I mind not publicly revealing the identity of the person who had taught me economics?

I've since reconsidered my views about emissions trading to some extent—though not for the doctrinal reasons the economists put forward. Unlike tossing litter out the car window onto the highway, emitting carbon dioxide is not in itself objectionable. We all do it every time we exhale. There's nothing intrinsically wrong with putting CO_2 into the air. What is objectionable is doing so in excess, as part of an energy-profligate way of life. That way of life, and the attitudes that support it, are what we should discourage, even stigmatize.[47]

One way of reducing pollution is by government regulation: require automakers to meet higher emissions standards; ban chemical companies and paper mills from dumping toxic waste into waterways; require factories to install scrubbers on their smokestacks. And if the companies fail to abide by the standards, fine them. That's what the United States did during the first generation of environmental laws, in the early 1970s.[48] The regulations, backed by fines, were a way of making companies pay for their pollution. They also carried a moral message: "Shame on us for spewing mercury and asbestos into lakes and streams and for befouling the air with choking smog. It's not only hazardous to our health; it's no way to treat the earth."

Some people opposed these regulations because they dislike anything that imposes higher costs on industry. But others, sympathetic to environmental protection, sought more efficient ways of achieving it. As the prestige of markets grew in the 1980s, and as economic ways of thinking deepened their hold, some environmental advocates began to favor market-based approaches to saving the planet. Don't impose emission standards on every factory, they reasoned; instead, put a price on pollution and let the market do the rest.[49]

The simplest way of putting a price on pollution is to tax it. A tax on emissions can be seen as a fee rather than a fine; but if it's big enough, it has the virtue of making the polluters pay for the damage they inflict. Precisely for this reason, it is politically difficult to enact. So policy makers have embraced a more market-friendly solution to pollution—emissions trading.

In 1990, President George H. W. Bush signed into law a plan to reduce acid rain, which is caused by sulfur dioxide emissions from coal-burning power plants. Rather than set fixed limits for each power plant, the law gave each utility company a license to pollute a certain amount, and then let the companies buy and sell the licenses among themselves. So a company could either reduce its own emissions or buy extra pollution permits from a company that had managed to pollute less than its allotted amount.[50]

Sulfur emissions declined, and the trading scheme was widely regarded as a success.[51] Then, later in the 1990s, attention turned to global warming. The Kyoto Protocol on climate change gave countries a choice: they could reduce their own greenhouse gas emissions or pay another country to reduce theirs. The rationale of this approach is that it reduces the cost of complying. If it's cheaper to replace kerosene lamps in Indian villages than to abate emissions in the United States, why not pay to replace the lamps?

Despite this inducement, the United States did not join the Kyoto agreement, and subsequent global climate talks have foundered. But my interest is less in the agreements themselves than in how they illustrate the moral costs of a global market in the right to pollute.

With the proposed market in procreation permits, the moral problem is that the system prompts some couples to bribe others to relinquish their chance to have a child. This erodes the norm of parental love, by encouraging parents to regard children as alienable, as commodities for sale. The moral problem with a global market in pollution permits is different. Here, the issue is not bribery but the outsourcing of an obligation. It arises more acutely in a global setting than in a domestic one.

Where global cooperation is at stake, allowing rich countries to avoid meaningful reductions in their own energy use by buying the right to pollute from others (or paying for programs that enable other countries to pollute less) does damage to two norms: it entrenches an instrumental attitude toward nature, and it undermines the spirit of shared sacrifice that may be necessary to create a global environmental ethic. If wealthy nations can buy their way out of an obligation to reduce their own carbon emissions, then the image of the hiker in the Grand Canyon may be apt after all. Only now, rather than pay a fine for littering, the wealthy hiker can toss his beer can with impunity, provided he hires someone to clean up litter in the Himalayas.

True, the two cases are not identical. Litter is less fungible than greenhouse gases. The beer can in the Grand Canyon is not offset by a pristine landscape half a world away. Global warming, by contrast, is a cumulative harm. From the standpoint of the heavens, it doesn't matter which places on the planet send less carbon to the sky.

But it does matter morally and politically. Letting rich countries buy their way out of meaningful changes in their own wasteful habits reinforces a bad attitude—that nature is a dumping ground for those who can afford it. Economists often assume that solving global warming is simply a matter of designing the right incentive structure and getting countries to sign on. But this misses a crucial point: norms matter. Global action on climate change may require that we find our way to a new environmental ethic, a new set of attitudes toward the natural world we share. Whatever its efficiency, a global market in the right to pollute may make it harder to cultivate the habits of restraint and shared sacrifice that a responsible environmental ethic requires.

Carbon Offsets

The growing use of voluntary carbon offsets raises a similar question. Oil companies and airlines now invite customers to make a monetary payment to neutralize their personal contribution to global warming. British Petroleum's website enables customers to calculate the amount of CO_2 their driving habits produce and to offset their emissions by making a financial contribution to green energy projects in the developing world. According to the website, the average British driver can offset a year's worth of emissions for about £20. British Airways offers a similar calculation. For a payment of $16.73, you can neutralize your share of the greenhouse gases produced by a round-trip flight between New York and London. The airline will remedy the damage your flight does to the heavens by sending your $16.73 to a wind farm in Inner Mongolia.[52]

Carbon offsets reflect a laudable impulse: to put a price on the damage our energy use inflicts upon the planet, and to pay the price, person by person, of setting it right. Raising funds to support reforestation and clean energy projects in the developing world is certainly worthwhile. But offsets also pose a danger: that those who buy them will consider themselves absolved of any further responsibility for climate change. The risk is that carbon offsets will become, at least for some, a painless mechanism to buy our way out of the more fundamental changes in habits, attitudes, and ways of life that may be required to address the climate problem.[53]

Critics of carbon offsets have compared them to indulgences, the monetary payments sinners paid the medieval church to offset their transgressions. A website called www.cheatneutral.com parodies carbon offsets by arranging the purchase and sale of offsets for infidelity. If someone in London feels guilty for cheating on his (or her) spouse, he can pay someone in Manchester to be faithful, thus "offsetting" the transgression. The moral analogy isn't perfect: Betrayal isn't objectionable only, or mainly, because it increases the sum of unhappiness in the world; it's a wrong to a particular person that can't be set right by a virtuous act elsewhere. Carbon emissions, by contrast, are not wrong as such, only in the aggregate.[54]

Still, the critics have a point. Commodifying and individuating responsibility for greenhouse gases could have the same paradoxical effect as charging for late pickups at the day-care center, producing more bad behavior rather than less. Here's how: In a time of global warming, driving a Hummer is seen as less a status symbol than a sign of wasteful self-indulgence, a kind of gluttony. Hybrids, by contrast, have a certain cachet. But carbon offsets could undermine these norms by seeming to confer a moral license to pollute. If Hummer drivers can assuage their guilt by writing a check to an organization that plants trees in Brazil, they may be less likely to trade in their gas-guzzler for a hybrid. Hummers may seem respectable rather than irresponsible, and the pressure for broader, collective responses to climate change could recede.

The scenario I've described is speculative, of course. The effects on norms of fines, fees, and other monetary incentives cannot be predicted with certainty and vary from case to case. My point is simply that markets reflect and promote certain norms, certain ways of valuing the goods they exchange. In deciding whether to commodify a good, we must therefore consider more than efficiency and distributive justice. We must also ask whether market norms will crowd out nonmarket norms, and if so, whether this represents a loss worth caring about.

I do not claim that promoting virtuous attitudes toward the environment, or parenting, or education must always trump competing considerations. Bribery sometimes works. And it may, on occasion, be the right thing to do. If paying underachieving kids to read books brings a dramatic improvement in reading skills, we might decide to try it, hoping we can teach them to love learning later. But it is important to remember that it is bribery we are engaged in, a morally compromised practice that substitutes a lower norm (reading to make money) for a higher one (reading for the love of it).

As markets and market-oriented thinking reach into spheres of life traditionally governed by nonmarket norms—health, education, procreation, refugee policy, environmental protection—this dilemma arises more and more often. What should we do when the promise of economic growth or economic efficiency means putting a price on goods we consider priceless? Sometimes, we find ourselves torn about whether to traffic in morally questionable markets in hopes of achieving worthy ends.

PAYING TO HUNT A RHINO

Suppose the goal is protecting endangered species—the black rhino, for example. From 1970 to 1992, Africa's population of black rhinos fell from sixty-five thousand to fewer than twenty-five hundred. Although hunting endangered species is illegal, most African countries were unable to protect rhinos from poachers, who sold their horns for great sums in Asia and the Middle East.[55]

In the 1990s and early 2000s, some wildlife conservation groups and South African biodiversity officials began to consider using market incentives to protect endangered species. If private ranchers were allowed to sell hunters the right to shoot and kill a limited number of black rhinos, the ranchers would have an incentive to breed them, care for them, and fend off poachers.

In 2004, the South African government won approval from the Convention on International Trade in Endangered Species to license five black rhino hunts. Black rhinos are notoriously dangerous and difficult animals to kill, and the chance to hunt one is highly prized among trophy hunters. The first legal hunt in decades commanded a handsome fee: $150,000, paid by an American hunter in the financial industry. Subsequent customers included a Russian petroleum billionaire, who paid to kill three black rhinos.

The market solution seems to be working. In Kenya, where the hunting of rhinos is still prohibited, the population of black rhinos has fallen from twenty thousand to about six hundred, as land is cleared of native vegetation and converted to agriculture and cattle farming. However, in South Africa, where landowners now have a monetary incentive to devote large ranches to wildlife, the black rhino population has begun to rebound.

For those who are untroubled by trophy hunting, selling the right to kill a black rhino is a sensible way of using market incentives to rescue an endangered species. If hunters are willing to pay $150,000 to hunt a rhino, ranchers have an incentive to raise rhinos and protect them, thus increasing supply. It's ecotourism with a twist: "Come pay to shoot an endangered black rhino. You'll have an unforgettable experience and serve the cause of conservation at the same time."

From the standpoint of economic reasoning, the market solution seems a clear winner. It makes some people better off and no one worse off. The ranchers make money, the hunters have a chance to stalk and shoot a formidable creature, and an endangered species is brought back from the brink of extinction. Who could complain?

Well, it depends on the moral status of trophy hunting. If you believe it's morally objectionable to kill wildlife for sport, the market in rhino hunts is a devil's bargain, a kind of moral extortion. You might welcome its good effect on rhino conservation but deplore the fact that this result is achieved by catering to what you consider the perverse pleasures of wealthy hunters. It would be like saving an ancient redwood forest from destruction by allowing loggers to sell wealthy donors the right to carve their initials in some of the trees.

So what should be done? You might reject the market solution on the grounds that the moral ugliness of trophy hunting trumps the conservation benefits. Or you might decide to pay the moral extortion and sell the right to hunt some rhinos in hopes of saving the species from extinction. The right answer partly depends on whether the market really will deliver the benefits it promises. But it also depends on whether trophy hunters are wrong to treat wildlife as an object of sport, and if so, on the moral gravity of that wrong.

Once again, we find that market reasoning is incomplete without moral reasoning. We can't decide whether to buy and sell the right to shoot rhinos without resolving the moral question about the proper way of valuing them. This is, of course, a contested question on which people disagree. But the case for markets cannot be disentangled from controversial questions about the right way to value the goods we exchange.

Big-game hunters instinctively grasp this point. They understand that the moral legitimacy of their sport (and of paying to hunt rhinos) depends on a certain view about the proper way of regarding wildlife. Some trophy hunters claim to venerate their prey, and maintain that killing a great and powerful creature is a form of respect. A Russian businessman who paid to hunt a black rhino in 2007 said, "I shot it because it was one of the biggest compliments I could give to the black rhino."[56] Critics will say that killing a creature is an odd way of venerating it. Whether trophy hunting values wildlife in an appropriate way is a moral question at the heart of the debate. Which brings us back to attitudes and norms: Whether to create a market in the hunting of endangered species depends not only on whether it increases their number but also on whether it expresses and promotes the right way of valuing them.

The black rhino market is morally complex because it seeks to protect an endangered species by promoting questionable attitudes toward wildlife. Here is another hunting story that poses an even tougher test for market reasoning.

PAYING TO SHOOT A WALRUS

For centuries, the Atlantic walrus was as abundant in the Arctic region of Canada as the bison in the American West. Valued for its meat, skin, blubber oil, and ivory tusks, the massive, defenseless marine mammal was easy prey for hunters, and by the late nineteenth century the population had been decimated. In 1928, Canada banned walrus hunting, with a small exception for the Inuit, aboriginal subsistence hunters whose way of life had revolved around the walrus hunt for forty-five hundred years.[57]

In the 1990s, Inuit leaders approached the Canadian government with a proposal. Why not allow the Inuit to sell the right to kill some of their walrus quota to big-game hunters? The number of walruses killed would remain the same. The Inuit would collect the hunting fees, serve as guides to the trophy hunters, supervise the kill, and keep the meat and skins as they had always done. The scheme would improve the economic well-being of a poor community without exceeding the existing quota. The Canadian government agreed.

Today, rich trophy hunters from around the world make their way to the Arctic for the chance to shoot a walrus. They pay $6,000 to $6,500 for the privilege. They do not come for the thrill of the chase or the challenge of stalking an elusive prey. Walruses are unthreatening creatures that move slowly and are no match for hunters with guns. In a compelling account in *The New York Times Magazine*, C. J. Chivers compared walrus hunting under Inuit supervision to "a long boat ride to shoot a very large beanbag chair."[58]

The guides maneuver the boat to within fifteen yards of the walrus and tell the hunter when to shoot. Chivers described the scene as a game hunter from Texas shot his prey: The hunter's "bullet smacked the bull on the neck, jerking its head and knocking the animal to its side. Blood spouted from the entry hole. The bull lay motionless. [The hunter] put down his rifle and picked up his video camera." The Inuit crew then set about the hard work of pulling the dead walrus onto an ice floe and carving up the carcass.

The appeal of such a hunt is difficult to fathom. It involves no challenge, making it less a sport than a kind of lethal tourism. The hunter cannot even display the remains of his prey on his trophy wall back home. Walruses are protected in the United States, and it's illegal to bring their body parts into the country.

So why shoot a walrus? Apparently, to fulfill the goal of killing one specimen of every creature on lists provided by hunting clubs—for example, the African "Big Five" (leopard, lion, elephant, rhino, and Cape buffalo) or the Arctic "Grand Slam" (caribou, musk ox, polar bear, and walrus).

It's hardly an admirable goal; many people find it repugnant. But remember, markets don't pass judgment on the desires they satisfy. In fact, from the standpoint of market reasoning, there's much to be said for allowing the Inuit to sell their right to shoot a certain number of walruses. The Inuit gain a new source of income, and the "list hunters" gain the chance to complete their roster of creatures killed, all without exceeding the existing quota. In this respect, selling the right to kill a walrus is like selling the right to procreate or to pollute.

Once you have a quota, market logic dictates that allowing tradable permits improves the general welfare. It makes some people better off without making anyone worse off.

And yet there is something morally disagreeable about the market in walrus killing. Let's assume, for the sake of argument, that it is reasonable to permit the Inuit to carry on with subsistence walrus hunting, as they've done for centuries. Allowing them to sell the right to kill walruses is still morally objectionable, for two reasons.

One is that this bizarre market caters to a perverse desire that should carry no weight in any calculus of social utility. Whatever one thinks of big-game hunting, this is something else. The desire to kill a helpless mammal at close range, without any challenge or chase, simply to complete a list, is not worthy of being fulfilled, even if doing so provides extra income for the Inuit. Second, for the Inuit to sell outsiders the right to kill their allotted walruses corrupts the meaning and purpose of the exemption accorded their community in the first place. It's one thing to honor the Inuit way of life and to respect its long-standing reliance on subsistence walrus hunting. It's quite another to convert that privilege into a cash concession in killing on the side.

INCENTIVES AND MORAL ENTANGLEMENTS

During the second half of the twentieth century, Paul Samuelson's *Economics* was the leading economics textbook in the country. I recently looked at an early (1958) edition of his book to see what he took economics to be. He identified economics with its traditional subject matter: "the world of prices, wages, interest rates, stocks and bonds, banks and credit, taxes and expenditure." The task of economics was concrete and circumscribed: to explain how depressions, unemployment, and inflation can be avoided, to study the principles "that tell us how productivity can be kept high" and "how people's standards of living can be improved."[59]

Today, economics has wandered quite a distance from its traditional subject matter. Consider this definition of an economy offered by Greg Mankiw in a recent edition of his own influential economics textbook: "There is no mystery to what an 'economy' is. An economy is just a group of people interacting with one another as they go about their lives."

In this account, economics is about not only the production, distribution, and consumption of material goods but also about human interaction in general and the principles by which individuals make decisions. One of the most important of these principles, Mankiw observes, is that "people respond to incentives."[60]

Talk of incentives has become so pervasive in contemporary economics that it has come to define the discipline. In the opening pages of *Freakonomics*, Steven D. Levitt, an economist at the University of Chicago, and Stephen J. Dubner declare that "incentives are the cornerstone of modern life" and that "economics is, at root, the study of incentives."[61]

It is easy to miss the novelty of this definition. The language of incentives is a recent development in economic thought. The word "incentive" does not appear in the writings of Adam Smith or other classical economists.[62] In fact, it didn't enter economic discourse until the twentieth century and didn't become prominent until the 1980s and 1990s. *The Oxford English Dictionary* finds its first use in the context of economics in 1943, in *Reader's Digest*: "Mr. Charles E. Wilson . . . is urging war industries to adopt 'incentive pay'—that is, to pay workers more if they *produce* more." The use of the word "incentives" rose sharply in the second half of the twentieth century, as markets and market thinking deepened their hold. According to a Google book search, the incidence of the term increased by over 400 percent from the 1940s to the 1990s.[63]

Conceiving economics as the study of incentives does more than extend the reach of markets into everyday life. It also casts the economist in an activist role. The "shadow" prices that Gary Becker invoked in the 1970s to explain human behavior were implicit, not actual. They were metaphorical prices that the economist imagines, posits, or infers. Incentives, by contrast, are interventions that the economist (or policy maker) designs, engineers, and imposes on the world. They are ways of getting people to lose weight, or work harder, or pollute less. "Economists love incentives," write Levitt and Dubner. "They love to dream them up and enact them, study them and tinker with them. The typical economist believes the world has not yet invented a problem that he cannot fix if given a free hand to design the proper incentive scheme. His solution may not always be pretty—it may involve coercion or exorbitant penalties or the violation of civil liberties—but the original problem, rest assured, will be fixed. An incentive is a bullet, a lever, a key: an often tiny object with astonishing power to change a situation."[64]

This is a far cry from Adam Smith's image of the market as an invisible hand. Once incentives become "the cornerstone of modern life," the market appears as a heavy hand, and a manipulative one. (Recall the cash incentives for sterilization and good grades.) "Most incentives don't come about organically," Levitt and Dubner observe. "Someone—an economist or a politician or a parent—has to invent them."[65]

The growing use of incentives in contemporary life, and the need for someone deliberately to invent them, is reflected in an ungainly new verb that has gained currency of late: "incentivize." According to the OED, to incentivize is "to motivate or encourage (a person, esp. an employee or customer) by providing a (usually financial) incentive." The word dates to 1968 but has become popular in the last decade, especially among economists, corporate executives, bureaucrats, policy analysts, politicians, and editorial writers. In books, the word scarcely appeared until around 1990. Since then, its use has soared by more than 1,400 percent.[66] A LexisNexis search of major newspapers reveals a similar trend:

Appearance of "incentivize" or "incentivise" in major newspapers[67]

1980s	48
1990s	449
2000s	6159
2010–11	5885

Recently, "incentivize" has entered the parlance of presidents. George H. W. Bush, the first U.S. president to use the term in public remarks, used it twice. Bill Clinton used it only once in eight years, as did George W. Bush. In his first three years in office, Barack Obama has used "incentivize" twenty-nine times. He hopes to incentivize doctors, hospitals, and health-care providers to give more attention to preventive care and wants "to poke, prod, [and] incentivize banks" to provide loans to responsible homeowners and small businesses.[68]

Britain's prime minister, David Cameron, is also fond of the word. Speaking to bankers and business leaders, he called for doing more to "incentivise" a "risk-taking investment culture." Speaking to the British people after the London riots of 2011, he complained that "some of the worst aspects of human nature" had been "tolerated, indulged, even sometimes incentivized," by the state and its agencies.[69]

Despite their new incentivizing bent, most economists continue to insist on the distinction between economics and ethics, between market reasoning and moral reasoning. Economics "simply doesn't traffic in morality," Levitt and Dubner explain. "Morality represents the way we would like the world to work, and economics represents how it actually does work."[70]

The notion that economics is a value-free science independent of moral and political philosophy has always been questionable. But the vaunting ambition of economics today makes this claim especially difficult to defend. The more markets extend their reach into noneconomic spheres of life, the more entangled they become with moral questions.

Consider economic efficiency. Why care about it? Presumably, for the sake of maximizing social utility, understood as the sum of people's preferences. As Mankiw explains, an efficient allocation of resources maximizes the economic well-being of all members of society.[71] Why maximize social utility? Most economists either ignore this question or fall back on some version of utilitarian moral philosophy.

But utilitarianism is open to some familiar objections. The objection most relevant to market reasoning asks why we should maximize the satisfaction of preferences regardless of their moral worth. If some people like opera and others like dogfights or mud wrestling, must we really be nonjudgmental and give these preferences equal weight in the utilitarian calculus?[72] When market reasoning is concerned with material goods, such as cars, toasters, and flat-screen televisions, this objection doesn't loom large; it's reasonable to assume that the value of the goods is simply a matter of consumer preference. But when market reasoning is applied to sex, procreation, child rearing, education, health, criminal punishment, immigration policy, and environmental protection, it's less plausible to assume that everyone's preferences are equally worthwhile. In morally charged arenas such as these, some ways of valuing goods may be higher, more appropriate than others. And if that's the case, it's unclear why we should satisfy preferences indiscriminately, without inquiring into their moral worth. (Should your desire to teach a child to read really count equally with your neighbor's desire to shoot a walrus at point-blank range?)

So when market reasoning travels beyond the domain of material goods, it must "traffic in morality," unless it wants blindly to maximize social utility without regard for the moral worth of the preferences it satisfies.

There's a further reason that the expansion of markets complicates the distinction between market reasoning and moral reasoning, between explaining the world and improving it. One of the central principles of economics is the price effect—when prices go up, people buy less of a good, and when prices go down, they buy more. This principle is generally reliable when we're talking about the market for, say, flat-screen TVs.

But as we've seen, it is less reliable when applied to social practices governed by nonmarket norms, like arriving on time to pick up your child at the day-care center. When the price of arriving late went up (from no charge), late pickups increased. This result confounds the standard price effect. But it's understandable if you recognize that marketizing a good can change its meaning. Putting a price on late pickups changed the norm. What was once seen as a moral obligation to arrive on time—to spare the teachers an inconvenience—was now seen as a market relationship, in which late-arriving parents could simply pay teachers for the service of staying longer. As a result, the incentive backfired.

The day-care story shows that, as markets reach into spheres of life governed by nonmarket norms, the standard price effect may not hold. Raising the (economic) cost of coming late led to more late pickups, not fewer. So to explain the world, economists have to figure out whether putting a price on an activity will crowd out nonmarket norms. To do so, they have to investigate the moral understandings that inform a given practice and determine whether marketizing the practice (by providing a financial incentive or disincentive) will displace them.

At this point, the economist might concede that, in order to explain the world, he or she must engage in moral psychology or anthropology, to figure out what norms prevail and how markets will affect them. But why does this mean that moral philosophy must enter the picture? For the following reason:

Where markets erode nonmarket norms, the economist (or someone) has to decide whether this represents a loss worth caring about. Should we care whether parents stop feeling guilty for picking up their children late and come to view their relationship with the teachers in more instrumental terms? Should we care if paying children to read books leads them to view reading as a job for pay and diminishes the joy of reading for its own sake? The answer will vary from case to case. But the question carries us beyond predicting whether a financial incentive will work. It requires that we make a moral assessment: What is the moral importance of the attitudes and norms that money may erode or crowd out? Would the loss of nonmarket norms and expectations change the character of the activity in ways we would (or at least should) regret? If so, should we avoid introducing financial incentives into the activity, even though they might do some good?

The answer will depend on the purpose and character of the activity in question and the norms that define it. Even day-care centers differ in this respect. Displacing shared expectations of mutual obligation may be more damaging in a cooperative, where parents volunteer a certain number of hours each week, than in a conventional day-care establishment, where parents pay the teachers to look after the children and then go about their day. But it is clear in any case that we are on moral terrain. To decide whether to rely on financial incentives, we need to ask whether those incentives will corrupt attitudes and norms worth protecting. To answer this question, market reasoning must become moral reasoning. The economist has to "traffic in morality" after all.

3

How Markets Crowd Out Morals

Are there some things that money should not be able to buy? If so, how can we decide which goods and activities are properly bought and sold, and which are not? I suggest we approach these questions by asking a slightly different one: Are there some things that money cannot buy?

WHAT MONEY CAN AND CANNOT BUY

Most people would say yes, there are. Consider friendship. Suppose you want more friends than you have. Would you try to buy some? Not likely. A moment's reflection would lead you to realize that it wouldn't work. A hired friend is not the same as a real one. You could hire people to do some of the things that friends typically do—picking up your mail when you're out of town, looking after your children in a pinch, or, in the case of a therapist, listening to your woes and offering sympathetic advice. Until recently, you could even bolster your online popularity by hiring some good-looking "friends" for your Facebook page—for 99¢ per friend per month. (The phony-friend website was shut down when it emerged that the photos being used, mostly of models, were unauthorized.)[1] Although all of these services can be bought, you can't actually buy a friend. Somehow, the money that buys the friendship dissolves it, or turns it into something else.

Or consider the Nobel Prize. Suppose you desperately want a Nobel Prize but fail to get one in the usual way. It might occur to you to buy one. But you would quickly realize that it wouldn't work. The Nobel Prize is not the kind of thing that money can buy. Nor is the Most Valuable Player award of the American League. You could buy the trophy if some previous winner is willing to sell it, and you could display it in your living room. But you could not buy the award itself.

This is not only because the Nobel committee and the American League don't offer these awards for sale. Even if they auctioned off, say, one Nobel Prize each year, the bought award would not be the same as the real thing. The market exchange would dissolve the good that gives the prize its value. This is because the Nobel Prize is an honorific good. To buy it is to undermine the good you are seeking. Once word got out that the prize had been bought, the award would no longer convey or express the honor and recognition that people receive when they are awarded a Nobel Prize.

The same is true of baseball's MVP awards. They too are honorific goods, whose value would be dissolved if bought rather than earned by a season of game-winning home runs or other heroics. There's a difference, of course, between a trophy, which symbolizes an award, and the award itself. It turns out that some winners of Hollywood's Academy Awards have sold their Oscar statuettes, or left them to heirs who have done so. Some of these Oscars have been auctioned by Sotheby's and other auction houses. In 1999, Michael

Jackson paid $1.54 million for the best-picture Oscar for *Gone with the Wind*. The academy that awards the Oscars opposes such sales and now requires Oscar recipients to sign an agreement promising not to sell them. It wants to avoid turning the iconic statuettes into commercial collectibles. Whether or not collectors are able to buy the trophies, it is obvious that buying the Academy Award for best actress is not the same as winning it.[2]

These fairly obvious examples offer a clue to the more challenging question that concerns us: Are there some things that money can buy but shouldn't? Consider a good that can be bought but whose buying and selling is morally controversial—a human kidney, for example. Some people defend markets in organs for transplantation; others find such markets morally objectionable. If it's wrong to buy a kidney, the problem is not, as with the Nobel Prize, that the money dissolves the good. The kidney will work (assuming a good match) regardless of the monetary payment. So to determine whether kidneys should or shouldn't be up for sale, we have to engage in a moral inquiry. We have to examine the arguments for and against organ sales and determine which are more persuasive.

Or consider baby selling. Some years ago, Judge Richard Posner, a leading figure in the "law and economics" movement, proposed the use of markets to allocate babies put up for adoption. He acknowledged that more desirable babies would command higher prices than less desirable ones. But he argued that the free market would do a better job of allocating babies than the current system of adoption, which allows adoption agencies to charge certain fees but not to auction babies or charge a market price.[3]

Many people disagree with Posner's proposal and maintain that children should not be bought and sold, no matter how efficient the market. In thinking through this controversy, it's worth noticing a distinctive feature of it: like a markets in kidneys, a market in babies would not dissolve the good the buyers seek to acquire. A bought baby differs, in this respect, from a bought friend or Nobel Prize. If there were a market in babies for adoption, people who paid the going price would acquire what they wanted—a child. Whether such a market is morally objectionable is a further question.

So it seems, at first glance, that there is a sharp distinction between two kinds of goods: the things (like friends and Nobel Prizes) that money *can't* buy, and the things (like kidneys and children) that money *can* buy but arguably shouldn't. But I would like to suggest that this distinction is less clear than it first appears. If we look more closely, we can glimpse a connection between the obvious cases, in which the monetary exchange spoils the good being bought, and the controversial cases, in which the good survives the selling but is arguably degraded, or corrupted, or diminished as a result.

BOUGHT APOLOGIES AND WEDDING TOASTS

We can explore this connection by considering some cases intermediate between friendship and kidneys. If you can't buy friendship, what about tokens of friendship, or expressions of intimacy, affection, or contrition?

In 2001, *The New York Times* published a story about a company in China that offers an unusual service: if you need to apologize to someone—an estranged lover or business partner with whom you've had a falling out—and you can't quite bring yourself to do so in person, you can hire the Tianjin Apology company to apologize on your behalf. The motto of the company is, "We say sorry for you." According to the article, the professional apologizers are "middle-aged men and women with college degrees who dress in somber suits. They are lawyers, social workers and teachers with 'excellent verbal ability' and significant life experience, who are given additional training in counseling."[4]

I don't know whether the company is successful, or even whether it still exists. But reading about it made me wonder: Does a bought apology work? If someone wronged or offended you, and then sent a hired apologizer to make amends, would you be satisfied? It might depend on the circumstances, or perhaps even the cost. Would you consider an expensive apology more meaningful than a cheap one? Or is the enactment of the apology by the person who owes it constitutive of contrition, such that it can't be outsourced? If no bought apology, however extravagant, could do the work of a personal one, then apologies, like friends, are the kind of thing that money cannot buy.

Consider another social practice closely connected to friendship—a wedding toast to the bride and groom. Traditionally, such toasts are warm, funny, heartfelt expressions of good wishes delivered by the best man, usually the groom's closest friend. But it's not easy to compose an elegant wedding speech, and many best men don't feel up to the task. So some have resorted to buying wedding toasts online.[5]

ThePerfectToast.com is one of the leading websites offering ghostwritten wedding speeches. It's been in business since 1997. You answer a questionnaire online—about how the bride and groom met, how you would describe them, whether you want a humorous speech or a sentimental one—and within three business days you receive a professionally written custom toast of three to five minutes. The price is $149, payable by credit card. For those who can't afford a bespoke wedding toast, other websites, such as InstantWedding-Toasts.com, sell standard prewritten wedding speeches for $19.95, including a money-back guarantee.[6]

Suppose, on your wedding day, your best man delivers a heart-warming toast, a speech so moving it brings tears to your eyes. You later learn that he didn't write it himself but bought it online. Would you care? Would the toast mean less than it did at first, before you knew it was written by a paid professional? Most of us would probably say yes, the bought wedding toast has less value than an authentic one.

It might be argued that presidents and prime ministers routinely employ speechwriters, and no one faults them for it. But a wedding toast is not a State of the Union address. It is an expression of friendship. Although a bought toast might "work" in the sense of achieving its desired effect, that effect might depend on an element of deception. Here's a test: If, seized with anxiety at the prospect of giving a speech at your best friend's wedding, you purchased a moving, sentimental masterpiece online, would you reveal this fact, or try to cover it up? If a bought toast depends for its effect on concealing its provenance, that's a reason to suspect it's a corrupt version of the real thing.

Apologies and wedding toasts are goods that can, in a sense, be bought. But buying and selling them changes their character and diminishes their value.

THE CASE AGAINST GIFTS

Consider now another expression of friendship—gift giving. Unlike wedding speeches, gifts have an unavoidably material aspect. But with some gifts, the monetary aspect is relatively obscure; with others, it is explicit. Recent decades have brought a trend toward the monetization of gifts, yet another example of the increasing commodification of social life.

Economists don't like gifts. Or to be more precise, they have a hard time making sense of gift giving as a rational social practice. From the standpoint of market reasoning, it is almost always better to give cash rather than a gift. If you assume that people generally know their own preferences best, and that the point of giving a gift is to make your friend or loved one happy, then it's hard to beat a monetary payment. Even if you have exquisite taste, your friend may not like the tie or necklace you pick out. So if you really want to maximize the welfare your gift provides, don't buy a present; simply give the money you would have spent. Your friend or lover can either spend the cash on the item you would have bought, or (more likely) on something that brings even greater pleasure.

This is the logic of the economic case against gift giving. It is subject to a few qualifications. If you come across an item that your friend would like but is unfamiliar with—the latest high-tech gadget, for example—it's possible this gift would give your ill-informed friend more pleasure than something he or she would have bought with the cash equivalent. But this is a special case that is consistent with the economist's basic assumption that the purpose of gift giving is to maximize the welfare, or utility, of the recipient.

Joel Waldfogel, an economist at the University of Pennsylvania, has taken up the economic inefficiency of gift giving as a personal cause. By "inefficiency," he means the gap between the value to you (maybe very little) of the $120 argyle sweater your aunt gave you for your birthday, and the value of what you would have bought (an iPod, say) had she given you the cash. In 1993, Waldfogel drew attention to the epidemic of squandered utility associated with holiday gift giving in an article called "The Deadweight Loss of Christmas." He updated and elaborated the theme in a recent book, *Scroogenomics: Why You Shouldn't Buy Presents for the Holidays*: "The bottom line is that when other people do our shopping, for clothes or music or whatever, it's pretty unlikely that they'll choose as well as we would have chosen for ourselves. We can expect their choices, no matter how well intentioned, to miss the mark. Relative to how much satisfaction their expenditures could have given us, their choices destroy value."[7]

Applying standard market reasoning, Waldfogel concludes that it would be better, in most cases, to give cash: "Economic theory—and common sense—lead us to expect that buying stuff for ourselves will create more satisfaction, per euro, dollar, or shekel spent, than does buying stuff for others . . . Buying gifts typically destroys value and can only, in the unlikely best special case, be as good as giving cash."[8]

Beyond playing out the economic logic against gift giving, Waldfogel has conducted surveys to measure how much value this inefficient practice destroys. He asks gift recipients to estimate the monetary value of the gifts they've received, and the amount they would have been willing to pay for them. His conclusion: "We value items we receive as gifts 20 percent less, per dollar spent, than items we buy for ourselves." This 20 percent figure enables Waldfogel to estimate the total "value destruction" brought about, nationwide, by holiday gift giving: "Given the $65 billion in U.S. holiday spending per year, that means we get $13 billion less in satisfaction than we would receive if we spent that money the usual way—carefully, on ourselves. Americans celebrate the holidays with an orgy of value destruction."[9]

If gift giving is a massively wasteful and inefficient activity, why do we persist in it? It isn't easy to answer this question within standard economic assumptions. In his economics textbook, Gregory Mankiw tries gamely to do so. He begins by observing that "gift giving is a strange custom" but concedes that it's generally a bad idea to give your boyfriend or girlfriend cash instead of a birthday present. But why?

Mankiw's explanation is that gift giving is a mode of "signaling," an economist's term for using markets to overcome "information asymmetries." So, for example, a firm with a good product buys expensive advertising, not only to persuade customers directly but also to "signal" to them that it is confident enough in the quality of its product to undertake a costly advertising campaign. In a similar way, Mankiw suggests, gift giving serves a signaling function. A man contemplating a gift for his girlfriend "has private information that the girlfriend would like to know: Does he really love her? Choosing a good gift for her is a signal of his love." Since it takes time and effort to look for a gift, choosing an apt one is a way for him "to convey the private information of his love for her."[10]

This is a strangely wooden way to think about lovers and gifts. "Signaling" love is not the same as expressing it. To speak of signaling wrongly assumes that love is a piece of private information that one party reports to the other. If this were the case, then cash would work as well—the higher the payment, the stronger the signal, and the greater (presumably) the love. But love is not only, or mainly, a matter of private information. It is a way of being with and responding to another person. Giving, especially attentive giving, can be an expression of it. On the expressive account, a good gift not only aims to please, in the sense of satisfying the consumer preferences of the recipient. It also engages and connects with the recipient, in a way that reflects a certain intimacy. This is why thoughtfulness matters.

Not all gifts, of course, can be expressive in this way. If you are attending the wedding of a distant cousin, or the bar mitzvah of a business associate's child, it is probably better to buy something from the wedding registry or give cash. But to give money rather than a well-chosen gift to a friend, lover, or spouse is to convey a certain thoughtless indifference. It's like buying your way out of attentiveness.

Economists know that gifts have an expressive dimension, even if the tenets of their discipline can't account for it. "The economist in me says the best gift is cash," writes Alex Tabarrok, an economist and blogger. "The rest of me rebels." He offers a good counterexample to the utilitarian notion that the ideal gift is an item we would have bought for ourselves: Suppose someone gives you $100, and you buy a set of tires for your car. This is what maximizes your utility. Still, you might not be terribly happy if your lover gave you car tires for your birthday. In most cases, Tabarrok points out, we'd rather the gift giver buy us something less mundane, something we wouldn't buy for ourselves. From our intimates at least, we'd rather receive a gift that speaks to "the wild self, the passionate self, the romantic self."[11]

I think he's onto something. The reason gift giving is not always an irrational departure from efficient utility maximizing is that gifts aren't only about utility. Some gifts are expressive of relationships that engage, challenge, and reinterpret our identities. This is because friendship is about more than being useful to one another. It is also about growing in character and self-knowledge in the company of others. As Aristotle taught, friendship at its best has a formative, educative purpose. To monetize all forms of giving among friends can corrupt friendship by suffusing it with utilitarian norms.

Even economists who view gift giving in utilitarian terms can't help noticing that cash gifts are the exception, not the rule, especially among peers, spouses, and significant others. For Waldfogel, this is a source of the inefficiency he decries. So what, in his view, motivates people to persist in a habit that produces a massive destruction of value? It's simply the fact that cash is considered a "tacky gift" that carries a stigma. He does not ask whether people are right or wrong to regard cash gifts as tacky. Instead, he treats the stigma as a brute sociological fact of no normative significance apart from its unfortunate tendency to reduce utility.[12]

"The only reason that so much Christmas giving is in-kind rather than cash is the stigma of cash giving," Waldfogel writes. "If there were no stigma, then givers would give cash, and recipients would choose items that they really want, resulting in the most possible satisfaction given the amounts spent."[13] Stephen Dubner and Steven Levitt offer a similar view: the reluctance to give cash gifts is, for the most part, a "social taboo" that "crushes the economist's dream" of a "beautifully efficient exchange."[14]

The economic analysis of gift giving illustrates, in a small domain, two revealing features of market reasoning. First, it shows how market reasoning smuggles in certain moral judgments, despite its claim to be value neutral. Waldfogel doesn't assess the validity of the stigma against cash gifts; he never asks whether it might be justified. He simply assumes it is an irrational obstacle to utility, a "dysfunctional institution" that should ideally be overcome.[15] He doesn't consider the possibility that the stigma against monetary gifts may reflect norms worth preserving, such as norms of attentiveness bound up with friendship.

To insist that the purpose of all gifts is to maximize utility is to assume, without argument, that the utility-maximizing conception of friendship is morally the most appropriate one, and that the right way to treat friends is to satisfy their preferences—not to challenge or deepen or complicate them.

So the economic case against gift giving is not morally neutral. It presupposes a certain conception of friendship, one that many consider impoverished. And yet, whatever its moral deficiency, the economic approach to gift giving is gradually taking hold. This brings us to the second revealing feature of the gift example. Contestable though its moral assumptions may be, the economic way of thinking about gifts is coming to be true. Over the past two decades, the monetary aspect of gift giving has come closer to the surface.

MONETIZING GIFTS

Consider the rise of gift cards. Rather than search for just the right gift, holiday shoppers are increasingly giving certificates or cards with a certain monetary value that can be redeemed for merchandise at retail stores. Gift cards represent a halfway house between choosing a specific gift and giving cash. They make life easier for shoppers and give recipients a greater range of options. A $50 gift card from Target, Walmart, or Saks Fifth Avenue avoids the "value-destroying loss" of a sweater two sizes too small, by letting the recipient choose something he or she really wants. And yet it's somehow different from giving money. True, the recipient knows exactly how much you spent; the monetary value is explicit. But despite this fact, a gift card from a particular store carries less of a stigma than simply giving cash. Perhaps the element of thoughtfulness conveyed by the choice of an appropriate store eases the stigma, at least to some degree.

The trend toward the monetizing of holiday gifts gathered momentum in the 1990s, when growing numbers of shoppers began giving gift certificates. In the late 1990s, the shift to plastic gift cards with magnetic strips accelerated the trend. From 1998 to 2010, annual sales of gift cards increased almost eightfold, to more than $90 billion. According to consumer surveys, gift cards are now the most popular holiday gift request—ahead of clothing, video games, consumer electronics, jewelry, and other items.[16]

Traditionalists bemoan this trend. Judith Martin, the etiquette columnist known as Miss Manners, complains that gift cards have "taken the heart and soul out of the holiday. You're basically paying somebody—paying them to go away." Liz Pulliam Weston, a personal finance columnist, worries that "the art of gift-giving is quickly devolving into an entirely commercial exchange. How much longer," she asks, "until we simply start thrusting wads of dollar bills at each other?"[17]

From the standpoint of economic reasoning, the turn to gift cards is a step in the right direction. Going all the way to wads of dollar bills would be even better. The reason? Although gift cards reduce the "deadweight loss" of presents, they don't eliminate it entirely. Suppose your uncle gives you a $100 gift card redeemable at Home Depot. That would be better than a hundred-dollar tool kit you don't want. But if you are not keen on home improvement items, you'd rather have the cash. Money, after all, is like a gift card that is redeemable anywhere.

Not surprisingly, a market solution to this problem has already appeared. A number of online companies now buy gift cards for cash (at a price lower than their face value) and resell them. So, for example, a company called Plastic Jungle will buy your $100 Home Depot gift card for $80 and then resell it for $93. The discount rate varies according to the popularity of the store. For a $100 gift card from Walmart or Target, Plastic Jungle will pay $91. A $100 card from Barnes & Noble, sadly, yields only $77, slightly less than Burger King ($79).[18]

For economists concerned with the deadweight loss of gifts, this secondary market quantifies the utility loss you impose on recipients by giving gift cards rather than money: the higher the discount rate, the greater the gap between the value of a gift card and the value of cash. Of course, none of this captures the thoughtfulness and attentiveness that traditional gift giving expresses. These virtues are attenuated in the shift from presents to gift cards and, finally, to cash.

One economist who studies gift cards suggests a way to reconcile the economic efficiency of cash with the old-fashioned virtue of thoughtfulness: "Gift-givers planning on giving a gift card might want to bear in mind the possible benefit of a cash gift with a note to the recipient suggesting that the money could be spent at [insert the name of store here]—to add the thought that counts."[19]

Giving money along with a cheery note advising the recipient where to spend it is the ultimate deconstructed gift. It's like packaging the utilitarian component and the expressive norm in two separate boxes, tied together with a bow.

My favorite example of the commodification of gift giving is a recently patented system for electronic regifting. An article in *The New York Times* describes it as follows: Suppose your aunt gives you a fruitcake for Christmas. The fruitcake company sends you an email informing you of the thoughtful gift and giving you the option of accepting delivery, exchanging it for something else, or sending the fruitcake to an unsuspecting person on your gift list. Since the transaction takes place online, you don't have to bother repacking the item and taking it to the post office. If you opt for regifting, the new recipient is offered the same options. So it's possible that the unwanted fruitcake could ricochet its way indefinitely through cyberspace.[20]

One possible snafu: depending on the retailer's disclosure policy, each recipient on the fruitcake's journey might be able to learn of its itinerary. This could be embarrassing. Learning that the fruitcake had been cast aside by several previous recipients and was now being fobbed off on you would likely dampen your gratitude for the gift and dissolve its expressive value. It would be a bit like discovering that your best friend had purchased that heartwarming wedding toast online.

BOUGHT HONOR

Although money can't buy friendship, it can buy tokens and expressions of friendship—up to a point. As we've seen, converting apologies, wedding toasts, and gifts into commodities doesn't destroy them altogether. But it does diminish them. The reason it diminishes them is related to the reason that money can't buy friends: Friendship and the social practices that sustain it are constituted by certain norms, attitudes, and virtues. Commodifying these practices displaces these norms—sympathy, generosity, thoughtfulness, attentiveness—and replaces them with market values.

A hired friend is not the same as a real one; almost everyone can tell the difference. The only exception I can think of is Jim Carrey's character in the movie *The Truman Show*. The character lives his entire life in a seemingly halcyon town that, unbeknownst to him, is actually the set of a reality television show. It takes Carrey some time to figure out that his wife and his best friend are hired actors. But of course he didn't hire them; the television producer did.

The point of the friendship analogy is this: the reason we (normally) can't buy friends—the purchase would destroy the relationship—sheds light on how markets corrupt expressions of friendship. A bought apology or wedding toast, though recognizable as something akin to an authentic one, is nonetheless tainted and diminished. Money can buy these things, but only in somewhat degraded form.

Honorific goods are vulnerable to corruption in a similar way. A Nobel Prize can't be bought. But what about other forms of honor and recognition? Consider honorary degrees. Colleges and universities confer honorary degrees on distinguished scholars, scientists, artists, and public officials. But some recipients are philanthropists who have contributed large sums to the institution bestowing the honor. Are such degrees bought, in effect, or are they genuinely honorific?

It can be ambiguous. If the college's reasons were baldly stated, the transparency would dissolve the good. Suppose the citation at commencement read: "We confer honorary degrees upon distinguished scientists and artists for their achievements. But we award you this degree in thanks for the $10 million you gave us to build a new library." Such an award would scarcely count as an honorary degree. Of course, citations are never written that way. They speak of public service, philanthropic commitment, and dedication to the university's mission—an honorific vocabulary that blurs the distinction between an honorary degree and a bought one.

Similar questions can be asked about the buying and selling of admission to elite universities. Universities don't hold auctions for admission, at least not explicitly. Many selective colleges and universities could increase their revenues if they sold seats in the freshman class to the highest bidder. But even if they wanted to maximize revenue, universities would not auction off all the places. Doing so would reduce demand, not only by reducing academic quality but also by undermining the honorific aspect of admission. It would be hard to take pride in being admitted (or having your child admitted) to Stanford or Princeton if admission were routinely purchased and if this were widely known. At most, it would be the kind of pride associated with being able to buy a yacht.

Suppose, however, that most of the places were allocated according to merit, but a few were quietly made available for sale. And let's also suppose that many factors entered into admissions decisions—grades; SAT scores; extracurricular activities; racial, ethnic, and geographical diversity; athletic prowess; legacy status (being the child of an alumnus)—so that it was hard to tell, in any given case, which factors were decisive. Under conditions such as these, universities could sell some places to wealthy donors without undermining the honor that people associate with admission to a top school.

Critics of higher education claim that this scenario comes close to describing what actually goes on at many colleges and universities today. They describe "legacy preferences," the admissions edge given to children of alumni, as a form of affirmative action for the affluent. And they point to cases in which universities have relaxed their admissions standards for less than outstanding applicants whose parents, though not alumni, are wealthy and likely to make a substantial contribution to the school.[21] Defenders of these practices argue that private universities depend heavily on financial contributions from alumni and wealthy donors, and that such contributions enable universities to provide scholarships and financial aid to less affluent students.[22]

So, unlike the Nobel Prize, college admission is a good that can be bought and sold, provided the buying and selling take place discreetly. Whether colleges and universities should do so is a further question. The idea of selling admission is open to two objections. One is about fairness; the other is about corruption. The fairness objection says that admitting children of wealthy donors in exchange for a handsome donation to the college fund is unfair to applicants who lacked the good judgment to be born to affluent parents. This objection views a college education as a source of opportunity and access, and worries that giving an edge to children of the wealthy perpetuates social and economic inequality.

The corruption objection is about institutional integrity. This objection points out that higher education not only equips students for remunerative jobs; it also embodies certain ideals—the pursuit of truth, the promotion of scholarly and scientific excellence, the advancement of humane teaching and learning, the cultivation of civic virtue. Although all universities need money to pursue their ends, allowing fund-raising needs to predominate runs the risk of distorting these ends and corrupting the norms that give universities their reason for being. That the corruption objection is about integrity—the fidelity of an institution to its constitutive ideals—is suggested by the familiar charge of "selling out."

TWO OBJECTIONS TO MARKETS

These two kinds of arguments reverberate through debates about what money should and should not buy. The fairness objection asks about the inequality that market choices may reflect; the corruption objection asks about the attitudes and norms that market relations may damage or dissolve.[23]

Consider kidneys. It's true that money can buy one without ruining its value. But should kidneys be bought and sold? Those who say no typically object on one of two grounds: They argue that such markets prey upon the poor, whose choice to sell their kidneys may not be truly voluntary (the fairness argument). Or they argue that such markets promote a degrading, objectifying view of the human person, as a collection of spare parts (the corruption argument).

Or consider children. It would be possible to create a market in babies up for adoption. But should we? Those who object offer two reasons: One is that putting children up for sale would price less affluent parents out of the market, or leave them with the cheapest, least desirable children (the fairness argument). The other is that putting a price tag on children would corrupt the norm of unconditional parental love; the inevitable price differences would reinforce the notion that the value of a child depends on his or her race, sex, intellectual promise, physical abilities or disabilities, and other traits (the corruption argument).

It's worth taking a moment to clarify these two arguments for the moral limits of markets. The fairness objection points to the injustice that can arise when people buy and sell things under conditions of inequality or dire economic necessity. According to this objection, market exchanges are not always as voluntary as market enthusiasts suggest. A peasant may agree to sell his kidney or cornea to feed his starving family, but his agreement may not really be voluntary. He may be unfairly coerced, in effect, by the necessities of his situation.

The corruption objection is different. It points to the degrading effect of market valuation and exchange on certain goods and practices. According to this objection, certain moral and civic goods are diminished or corrupted if bought and sold. The argument from corruption cannot be met by establishing fair bargaining conditions. It applies under conditions of equality and inequality alike.

The long-standing debate about prostitution illustrates the difference. Some people oppose prostitution on the grounds that it is rarely, if ever, truly voluntary. They argue that those who sell their bodies for sex are typically coerced, whether by poverty, drug addiction, or the threat of violence. This is a version of the fairness objection. But others object to prostitution on the grounds that it is degrading to women, whether or not they are forced into it. According to this argument, prostitution is a form of corruption that demeans women and promotes bad attitudes toward sex. The degradation objection doesn't depend on tainted consent; it would condemn prostitution even in a society without poverty, even in cases of upscale prostitutes who liked the work and freely chose it.

Each objection draws on a different moral ideal. The fairness argument draws on the ideal of consent or, more precisely, the ideal of consent carried out under fair background conditions. One of the main arguments for using markets to allocate goods is that markets respect freedom of choice. They allow people to choose for themselves whether to sell this or that good at a given price.

But the fairness objection points out that some such choices are not truly voluntary. Market choices are not free choices if some people are desperately poor or lack the ability to bargain on fair terms. So in order to know whether a market choice is a free choice, we have to ask what inequalities in the background conditions of society undermine meaningful consent. At what point do inequalities of bargaining power coerce the disadvantaged and undermine the fairness of the deals they make?

The corruption argument points to a different set of moral ideals. It appeals not to consent but to the moral importance of the goods at stake, the ones said to be degraded by market valuation and exchange. So to decide whether college admission should be bought and sold, we have to debate the moral and civic goods that colleges should pursue, and ask whether selling admission would damage those goods. To decide whether to establish a market in babies up for adoption, we need to ask what norms should govern the parent-child relationship, and ask whether buying and selling children would undermine those norms.

The fairness and corruption objections differ in their implications for markets: The fairness argument does not object to marketizing certain goods on the grounds that they are precious or sacred or priceless; it objects to buying and selling goods against a background of inequality severe enough to create unfair bargaining conditions. It offers no basis for objecting to the commodification of goods (whether sex or kidneys or college admission) in a society whose background conditions are fair.

The corruption argument, by contrast, focuses on the character of the goods themselves and the norms that should govern them. So it cannot be met simply by establishing fair bargaining conditions. Even in a society without unjust differences of power and wealth, there would still be things that money should not buy. This is because markets are not mere mechanisms; they embody certain values. And sometimes, market values crowd out nonmarket norms worth caring about.

CROWDING OUT NONMARKET NORMS

How exactly does this crowding out take place? How do market values corrupt, dissolve, or displace nonmarket norms? Standard economic reasoning assumes that commodifying a good—putting it up for sale—does not alter its character. Market exchanges increase economic efficiency without changing the goods themselves. That is why economists are generally sympathetic to using financial incentives to elicit desirable behavior; scalping tickets for highly prized concerts, sporting events, even papal masses; employing tradable quotas to allocate pollution, refugees, and procreation; giving cash gifts rather than presents; using markets to ease the gap between supply and demand for all manner of goods, even kidneys. Market exchanges make both parties better off without making anyone else worse off—*if* you assume that market relations and the attitudes they foster don't diminish the value of the goods being exchanged.

But this assumption is open to doubt. We've already considered a raft of examples that call it into question. As markets reach into spheres of life traditionally governed by nonmarket norms, the notion that markets don't touch or taint the goods they exchange becomes increasingly implausible. A growing body of research confirms what common sense suggests: financial incentives and other market mechanisms can backfire by crowding out nonmarket norms. Sometimes, offering payment for a certain behavior gets you less of it, not more.

NUCLEAR WASTE SITES

For years, Switzerland had been trying to find a place to store radioactive nuclear waste. Although the country relies heavily on nuclear energy, few communities wanted nuclear waste to reside in their midst. One location designated as a potential nuclear waste site was the small mountain village of Wolfenschiessen (pop. 2,100), in central Switzerland. In 1993, shortly before a referendum on the issue, some economists surveyed the residents of the village, asking whether they would vote to accept a nuclear waste repository in their community, if the Swiss parliament decided to build it there. Although the facility was widely viewed as an undesirable addition to the neighborhood, a slim majority (51 percent) of residents said they would accept it. Apparently their sense of civic duty outweighed their concern about the risks. Then the economists added a sweetener: suppose parliament proposed building the nuclear waste facility in your community *and* offered to compensate each resident with an annual monetary payment. *Then* would you favor it?[24]

The result: support went down, not up. Adding the financial inducement cut the rate of acceptance in half, from 51 to 25 percent. The offer of money actually reduced people's willingness to host the nuclear waste site. What's more, upping the ante didn't help. When the economists increased the monetary offer, the result was unchanged. The residents stood firm even when offered yearly cash payments as high as $8,700 per person, well in excess of the median monthly income. Similar if less dramatic reactions to monetary offers have been found in other places where local communities have resisted radioactive waste repositories.[25]

So what was going on in the Swiss village? Why would more people accept nuclear waste for free than for pay?

Standard economic analysis suggests that offering people money to accept a burden would increase, not decrease their willingness to do so. But Bruno S. Frey and Felix Oberholzer-Gee, the economists who led the study, point out that the price effect is sometimes confounded by moral considerations, including a commitment to the common good. For many villagers, willingness to accept the nuclear waste site reflected public spirit—a recognition that the country as a whole depended on nuclear energy and that the nuclear waste had to be stored somewhere. If their community was found to be the safest storage site, they were willing to bear the burden. Against the background of this civic commitment, the offer of cash to residents of the village felt like a bribe, an effort to buy their vote. In fact, 83 percent of those who rejected the monetary proposal explained their opposition by saying they could not be bribed.[26]

You might think that adding a financial incentive would simply reinforce whatever public-spirited sentiment already exists, thus increasing support for the nuclear waste site. After all, aren't two incentives—one financial, the other civic—more powerful than one? Not necessarily. It is a mistake to assume that incentives are additive. To the contrary, for the good citizens of Switzerland, the prospect of a private payoff transformed a civic question into a pecuniary one. The intrusion of market norms crowded out their sense of civic duty.

"Where public spirit prevails," the authors of the study conclude, "using price incentives to muster support for the construction of a socially desirable, but locally unwanted, facility comes at a higher price than suggested by standard economic theory because these incentives tend to crowd out civic duty."[27]

This does not mean that government agencies should simply impose siting decisions on local communities. High-handed regulation can be even more corrosive of public spirit than monetary incentives. Enabling local residents to assess the risks for themselves, allowing citizens to participate in deciding what sites best serve the public interest, giving host communities the right to close dangerous facilities if necessary—these are surer ways of generating public support than simply trying to buy it.[28]

Although cash payoffs are generally resented, compensation in kind is often welcomed. Communities often accept compensation for the siting of undesirable public projects—an airport, a landfill site, a recycling station—in their own backyards. But studies have found that people are more likely to accept such compensation if it takes the form of public goods rather than cash. Public parks, libraries, school improvements, community centers, even jogging and bicycle trails are more readily accepted as compensation than are monetary payments.[29]

From the standpoint of economic efficiency, this is puzzling, even irrational. Cash is always better, supposedly, than in-kind public goods, for reasons we explored in connection with gift giving. Money is fungible, the universal gift card: if residents are compensated in cash, they can always decide to pool their windfall to pay for public parks, libraries, and playgrounds, if that is what will maximize their utility. Or they can choose to spend the money on private consumption.

But this logic misses the meaning of civic sacrifice. Public goods are more fitting than private cash as compensation for public harms and inconveniences, because such goods acknowledge the civic burdens and shared sacrifice that siting decisions impose. A monetary payment to residents for accepting a new runway or landfill in their town can be seen as a bribe to acquiesce in the degradation of the community. But a new library, playground, or school repays the civic sacrifice in the same coin, so to speak, by strengthening the community and honoring its public spirit.

DONATION DAY AND LATE PICKUPS

Financial incentives have also been found to crowd out public spirit in settings less fateful than those involving nuclear waste. Each year, on a designated "donation day," Israeli high school students go door-to-door to solicit donations for worthy causes—cancer research, aid to disabled children, and so on. Two economists did an experiment to determine the effect of financial incentives on the students' motivations.

They divided the students into three groups. One group was

given a brief motivational speech about the importance of the cause and sent on its way. The second and third groups were given the same speech but also offered a monetary reward based on the amount they collected—1 percent and 10 percent, respectively. The rewards would not be deducted from the charitable donations; they would come from a separate source.[30]

Which group of students do you think raised the most money? If you guessed the unpaid group, you are right. The unpaid students collected 55 percent more in donations than those who were offered a 1 percent commission. Those who were offered 10 percent did considerably better than the 1 percent group, but less well than the students who were not paid at all. (The unpaid volunteers collected 9 percent more than those on the high commission.)[31]

What's the moral of the story? The authors of the study conclude that, if you're going to use financial incentives to motivate people, you should either "pay enough or don't pay at all."[32] While it may be true that paying enough will get you what you want, that's not all this story tells us. There is also a lesson here about how money crowds out norms.

To a degree, the experiment confirms the familiar assumption that monetary incentives work. After all, the 10 percent group collected more in contributions than those who were offered only 1 percent. But the interesting question is why both paid groups lagged behind those doing it for free. Most likely, it was because paying students to do a good deed changed the character of the activity. Going door-to-door collecting funds for charity was now less about performing a civic duty and more about earning a commission. The financial incentive transformed a public-spirited activity into a job for pay. As with the Swiss villagers, so with the Israeli students: the introduction of market norms displaced, or at least dampened, their moral and civic commitment.

A similar lesson emerges from another notable experiment conducted by the same researchers—the one involving the Israeli day-care centers. As we've already seen, introducing a fine for parents who came late to pick up their children did not reduce the number of late-arriving parents, but increased it. In fact, the incidence of late pickups nearly doubled. The parents treated the fine as a fee they were willing to pay. Not only that: When, after about twelve weeks, the day-care centers eliminated the fine, the new, elevated rate of late arrivals persisted. Once the monetary payment had eroded the moral obligation to show up on time, the old sense of responsibility proved difficult to revive.[33]

These three cases—of nuclear waste siting, charitable fund-raising, and late day-care pickups—illustrate the way introducing money into a nonmarket setting can change people's attitudes and crowd out moral and civic commitments. The corrosive effect of market relations is sometimes strong enough to override the price effect: offering a financial incentive to accept a hazardous facility, or go door-to-door collecting charity, or show up on time reduced rather than increased people's willingness to do so.

Why worry about the tendency of markets to crowd out nonmarket norms? For two reasons: one fiscal, the other ethical. From an economic point of view, social norms such as civic virtue and public-spiritedness are great bargains. They motivate socially useful behavior that would otherwise cost a lot to buy. If you had to rely on financial incentives to get communities to accept nuclear waste, you'd have to pay a lot more than if you could rely instead on the residents' sense of civic obligation. If you had to hire schoolchildren to collect charitable donations, you'd have to pay more than a 10 percent commission to get the same result that public spirit produces for free.

But to view moral and civic norms simply as cost-effective ways of motivating people ignores the intrinsic value of the norms. (It's like treating the stigma against cash gifts as a social fact that stands in the way of economic efficiency but that can't be assessed in moral terms.) Relying solely on cash payments to induce residents to accept a nuclear waste facility is not only expensive; it is also corrupting. It bypasses persuasion and the kind of consent that arises from deliberating about the risks the facility poses and the larger community's need for it. In a similar way, paying students to collect contributions on donation day not only adds to the cost of fund-raising; it also dishonors their public spirit and disfigures their moral and civic education.

THE COMMERCIALIZATION EFFECT

Many economists now recognize that markets change the character of the goods and social practices they govern. In recent years, one of the first to emphasize the corrosive effect of markets on nonmarket norms was Fred Hirsch, a British economist who served as a senior adviser to the International Monetary Fund. In a book published in 1976—the same year that Gary Becker's influential *An Economic Approach to Human Behavior* appeared and three years before Margaret Thatcher was elected prime minister—Hirsch challenged the assumption that the value of a good is the same whether provided through the market or in some other way.

Hirsch argues that mainstream economics has overlooked what he calls the "commercialization effect." By this he means "the effect on the characteristics of a product or activity of supplying it exclusively or predominantly on commercial terms rather than on some other basis—such as informal exchange, mutual obligation, altruism or love, or feelings of service or obligation." The "common assumption, almost always hidden, is that the commercialization process does not affect the product." Hirsch observes that this mistaken assumption loomed large in the rising "economic imperialism" of the time, including attempts, by Becker and others, to extend economic analysis into neighboring realms of social and political life.[34]

Hirsch died just two years later, at the age of forty-seven, and so did not have the chance to elaborate his critique of mainstream economics. In the ensuing decades, his book became a minor classic among those who rejected the growing commodification of social life and the economic reasoning that propelled it. The three empirical cases we've just considered support Hirsch's insight—that the introduction of market incentives and mechanisms can change people's attitudes and crowd out nonmarket values. Recently, other empirically minded economists have been finding further evidence of the commercialization effect.

For example, Dan Ariely, one of a growing number of behavioral economists, did a series of experiments demonstrating that paying people to do something may elicit less effort from them than asking them to do it for free, especially if it's a good deed. He tells a real-life anecdote that illustrates his findings. The American Association of Retired Persons asked a group of lawyers if they would be willing to provide legal services to needy retirees at a discounted rate of $30 an hour. The lawyers refused. Then the AARP asked if they would provide legal advice to the needy retirees for free. The lawyers agreed. Once it was clear they were being asked to engage in a charitable activity rather than a market transaction, the lawyers responded charitably.[35]

A growing body of work in social psychology offers a possible explanation for this commercialization effect. These studies highlight the difference between intrinsic motivations (such as moral conviction or interest in the task at hand) and external ones (such as money or other tangible rewards). When people are engaged in an activity they consider intrinsically worthwhile, offering them money may weaken their motivation by depreciating or "crowding out" their intrinsic interest or commitment.[36] Standard economic theory construes all motivations, whatever their character or source, as preferences and assumes they are additive. But this misses the corrosive effect of money.

The crowding-out phenomenon has big implications for economics. It calls into question the use of market mechanisms and market reasoning in many aspects of social life, including financial incentives to motivate performance in education, health care, the workplace, voluntary associations, civic life, and other settings in which intrinsic motivations or moral commitments matter. Bruno Frey (an author of the Swiss nuclear waste siting study) and the economist Reto Jegen summarize the implications as follows: "Arguably, the 'crowding-out effect' is one of the most important anomalies in economics, as it suggests the opposite of the most fundamental economic 'law,' that raising monetary incentives increases supply. If the crowding-out effect holds, raising monetary incentives reduces, rather than increases, supply."[37]

BLOOD FOR SALE

Perhaps the best-known illustration of markets crowding out nonmarket norms is a classic study of blood donation by the British sociologist Richard Titmuss. In his 1970 book *The Gift Relationship*,

Titmuss compared the system of blood collection used in the United Kingdom, where all blood for transfusion is given by unpaid, voluntary donors, and the system in the United States, where some blood is donated and some bought by commercial blood banks from people, typically the poor, who are willing to sell their blood as a way of making money. Titmuss argued in favor of the U.K. system and against treating human blood as a commodity to be bought and sold on the market.

Titmuss presented a wealth of data showing that, in economic and practical terms alone, the British blood collection system works better than the American one. Despite the supposed efficiency of markets, he argued, the American system leads to chronic shortages, wasted blood, higher costs, and a greater risk of contaminated blood.[38] But Titmuss also leveled an ethical argument against the buying and selling of blood.

Titmuss's ethical argument against the commodification of blood offers a good illustration of the two objections to markets identified earlier—fairness and corruption. Part of his argument is that a market in blood exploits the poor (the fairness objection). He observed that for-profit blood banks in the United States recruit much of their supply from Skid Row residents desperate for quick cash. The commercialization of blood leads to more blood "being supplied by the poor, the unskilled, the unemployed, Negroes and other low income groups." A "new class is emerging of an exploited human population of high blood yielders," he wrote. The redistribution of blood "from the poor to the rich appears to be one of the dominant effects of the American blood banking systems."[39]

But Titmuss had a further objection: turning blood into a market commodity erodes people's sense of obligation to donate blood, diminishes the spirit of altruism, and undermines the "gift relationship" as an active feature of social life (the corruption objection). Looking at the United States, he lamented the "decline in recent years in the voluntary giving of blood," and attributed this to the rise of commercial blood banks. "Commercialization and profit in blood has been driving out the voluntary donor." Once people begin to view blood as a commodity that is routinely bought and sold, Titmuss suggested, they are less likely to feel a moral responsibility to donate it. Here he was pointing to the crowding-out effect of market relations on nonmarket norms, though he didn't use this phrase. The widespread buying and selling of blood demoralizes the practice of giving blood for free.[40]

Titmuss was concerned not only with the declining willingness to give blood but also with the broader moral implications. Beyond its harmful effect on the quantity and quality of blood, the declining spirit of giving made for an impoverished moral and social life. "It is likely that a decline in the spirit of altruism in one sphere of human activities will be accompanied by similar changes in attitudes, motives and relationships in other spheres."[41]

While a market-based system does not prevent anyone from donating blood if he or she wants to, the market values that suffuse the system exert a corrosive effect on the norm of giving. "The ways in which society organizes and structures its social institutions—and particularly its health and welfare systems—can encourage or discourage the altruistic in man; such systems can foster integration or alienation; they can allow the 'theme of the gift'—of generosity towards strangers—to spread among and between social groups and generations." At some point, Titmuss worried, market-driven societies might become so inhospitable to altruism that they could be said to impair the freedom of persons to give. The "commercialization of blood and donor relationships represses the expression of altruism," he concluded, and "erodes the sense of community."[42]

Titmuss's book prompted much debate. Among his critics was Kenneth Arrow, one of the most distinguished American economists of his time. Arrow was no Milton Friedman–like proponent of unfettered markets. His earlier work had analyzed imperfections in markets for health care. But he took strong exception to Titmuss's critique of economics and market thinking.[43] In doing so, Arrow invoked two key tenets of the market faith—two assumptions about human nature and moral life that economists often assert but rarely defend.

TWO TENETS OF MARKET FAITH

The first is that commercializing an activity doesn't change it. On this assumption, money never corrupts, and market relations never crowd out nonmarket norms. If this is true, then the case for extending markets into every aspect of life is hard to resist. If a previously untraded good is made tradable, no harm is done. Those who wish to buy and sell it can do so, thereby increasing their utility, while those who regard the good as priceless are free to desist from trafficking in it. According to this logic, allowing market transactions makes some people better off without making anyone else worse off—even if the good being bought and sold is human blood. As Arrow explains: "Economists typically take for granted that since the creation of a market increases the individual's area of choice it therefore leads to higher benefits. Thus, if to a voluntary blood donor system we add the possibility of selling blood, we have only expanded the individual's range of alternatives. If he derives satisfaction from giving, it is argued, he can still give, and nothing has been done to impair that right."[44]

This line of reasoning leans heavily on the notion that creating a market in blood does not change its value or meaning. Blood is blood, and it will serve its life-sustaining purpose whether gifted or sold. Of course, the good at stake here is not only blood but also the act of donating blood out of altruism. Titmuss attaches independent moral value to the generosity that motivates the gift. But Arrow doubts that even this practice could be damaged by the introduction of a market: "Why should it be that the creation of a market for blood would decrease the altruism embodied in giving blood?"[45]

The answer is that commercializing blood changes the meaning of donating it. For consider: In a world where blood is routinely bought and sold, is donating a pint of blood at your local Red Cross still an act of generosity? Or is it an unfair labor practice that deprives needy persons of gainful employment selling their blood? If you want to contribute to a blood drive, would it be better to donate blood yourself, or to donate $50 that can be used to buy an extra pint of blood from a homeless person who needs the income? A would-be altruist could be forgiven for being confused.

The second tenet of market faith that figures in Arrow's critique is that ethical behavior is a commodity that needs to be economized. The idea is this: we should not rely too heavily on altruism, generosity, solidarity, or civic duty, because these moral sentiments are scarce resources that are depleted with use. Markets, which rely on self-interest, spare us from using up the limited supply of virtue. So, for example, if we rely on the generosity of the public for the supply of blood, there will be less generosity left over for other social or charitable purposes. If, however, we use the price system to generate the blood supply, people's altruistic impulses will be available, undiminished, when we really need them. "Like many economists," Arrow writes, "I do not want to rely too heavily on substituting ethics for self-interest. I think it best on the whole that the requirement of ethical behavior be confined to those circumstances where the price system breaks down . . . We do not wish to use up recklessly the scarce resources of altruistic motivation."[46]

It is easy to see how this economistic conception of virtue, if true, provides yet further grounds for extending markets into every sphere of life, including those traditionally governed by nonmarket values. If the supply of altruism, generosity, and civic virtue is fixed, as if by nature, like the supply of fossil fuels, then we should try to conserve it. The more we use, the less we have. On this assumption, relying more on markets and less on morals is a way of preserving a scarce resource.

ECONOMIZING LOVE

The classic statement of this idea was offered by Sir Dennis H. Robertson, a Cambridge University economist and former student of John Maynard Keynes, in an address at the bicentennial of Columbia University in 1954. The title of Robertson's lecture was a question: "What does the economist economize?" He sought to show that, despite catering to "the aggressive and acquisitive instincts" of human beings, economists nonetheless serve a moral mission.[47]

Robertson began by conceding that economics, concerned as it is with the desire for gain, does not deal with the noblest human motives. "It is for the preacher, lay or clerical," to inculcate the higher virtues—altruism, benevolence, generosity, solidarity, and civic duty.

"It is the humbler, and often the invidious, role of the economist to help, so far as he can, in reducing the preacher's task to manageable dimensions."[48]

How does the economist help? By promoting policies that rely, whenever possible, on self-interest rather than altruism or moral considerations, the economist saves society from squandering its scarce supply of virtue. "If we economists do [our] business well," Robertson concludes, "we can, I believe, contribute mightily to the economizing . . . of that scarce resource Love," the "most precious thing in the world."[49]

To those not steeped in economics, this way of thinking about the generous virtues is strange, even far-fetched. It ignores the possibility that our capacity for love and benevolence is not depleted with use but enlarged with practice. Think of a loving couple. If, over a lifetime, they asked little of one another, in hopes of hoarding their love, how well would they fare? Wouldn't their love deepen rather than diminish the more they called upon it? Would they do better to treat one another in more calculating fashion, to conserve their love for the times they really needed it?

Similar questions can be asked about social solidarity and civic virtue. Should we try to conserve civic virtue by telling citizens to go shopping until their country needs to call upon them to sacrifice for the common good? Or do civic virtue and public spirit atrophy with disuse? Many moralists have taken the second view. Aristotle taught that virtue is something we cultivate with practice: "we become just by doing just acts, temperate by doing temperate acts, brave by doing brave acts."[50]

Rousseau held a similar view. The more a country asks of its citizens, the greater their devotion to it. "In a well-ordered city every man flies to the assemblies." Under a bad government, no one participates in public life "because no one is interested in what happens there" and "domestic cares are all-absorbing." Civic virtue is built up, not spent down, by strenuous citizenship. Use it or lose it, Rousseau says, in effect. "As soon as public service ceases to be the chief business of the citizens, and they would rather serve with their money than with their persons, the state is not far from its fall."[51]

Robertson offers his observation in a lighthearted, speculative spirit. But the notion that love and generosity are scarce resources that are depleted with use continues to exert a powerful hold on the moral imagination of economists, even if they don't argue for it explicitly. It is not an official textbook principle, like the law of supply and demand. No one has proved it empirically. It is more like an adage, a piece of folk wisdom, to which many economists still subscribe.

Almost half a century after Robertson's lecture, the economist Lawrence Summers, then the president of Harvard University, was invited to offer the morning prayer in Harvard's Memorial Church. He chose as his theme what "economics can contribute to thinking about moral questions." Economics, he stated, "is too rarely appreciated for its moral as well as practical significance."[52]

Summers observed that economists place "great emphasis on respect for individuals—and the needs, tastes, choices and judgment they make for themselves." He then offered a standard utilitarian account of the common good as the sum of people's subjective preferences: "It is the basis of much economic analysis that the good is an aggregation of many individuals' assessments of their own well-being, and not something that can be assessed" apart from these preferences on the basis of an independent moral theory.

He illustrated this approach by challenging students who had advocated a boycott of goods produced by sweatshop labor: "We all deplore the conditions in which so many on this planet work and the paltry compensation they receive. And yet there is surely some moral force to the concern that as long as the workers are voluntarily employed, they have chosen to work because they are working to their best alternative. Is narrowing an individual's set of choices an act of respect, of charity, even of concern?"

He concluded with a reply to those who criticize markets for relying on selfishness and greed: "We all have only so much altruism in us. Economists like me think of altruism as a valuable and rare good that needs conserving. Far better to conserve it by designing a system in which people's wants will be satisfied by individuals being selfish, and saving that altruism for our families, our friends, and the many social problems in this world that markets cannot solve."

Here was Robertson's adage reasserted. Notice that Summers's version of it is even starker than Arrow's: Reckless expenditures of altruism in social and economic life not only deplete the supply available for other public purposes. They even reduce the amount we have left for our families and friends.

This economistic view of virtue fuels the faith in markets and propels their reach into places they don't belong. But the metaphor is misleading. Altruism, generosity, solidarity, and civic spirit are not like commodities that are depleted with use. They are more like muscles that develop and grow stronger with exercise. One of the defects of a market-driven society is that it lets these virtues languish. To renew our public life we need to exercise them more strenuously.

4

Markets in Life and Death

Michael Rice, forty-eight, an assistant manager at a Walmart in Tilton, New Hampshire, was helping a customer carry a television to her car when he had a heart attack and collapsed. He died a week later. An insurance policy on his life paid out about $300,000. But the money did not go to his wife and two children. It went to Walmart, which had purchased the policy on Rice's life and named itself as the beneficiary.[1]

When his widow, Vicki Rice, learned of Walmart's windfall, she was outraged. Why should the company be able to profit from her husband's death? He had worked long hours for the company, sometimes as much as eighty hours a week. "They used Mike terribly," she said, "and then they go out and collect $300,000? It's very immoral."[2]

According to Mrs. Rice, neither she nor her husband had any idea that Walmart had taken out a life insurance policy on him. When she learned of the policy, she sued Walmart in federal court, claiming that the money should go to the family, not the company. Her attorney argued that corporations should not be able to profit from the death of their workers: "It is absolutely reprehensible for a giant like Wal-Mart to be gambling on the lives of its employees."[3]

A Walmart spokesman acknowledged that the company held life insurance policies on hundreds of thousands of its employees—not only on assistant managers but even on maintenance workers. But he denied that this amounted to profiting from death. "It is our contention that we did not benefit from the death of our associates," he said. "We had a considerable investment in these employees" and came out ahead "if they continued to live." In the case of Michael Rice, the spokesman argued, the insurance payout was not a welcome windfall but compensation for the cost of training him and, now, of replacing him. "He had been given quite a bit of training and gained experiences that cannot be duplicated without costs."[4]

JANITORS INSURANCE

It has long been common practice for companies to take out insurance on the lives of their CEOs and top executives, to offset the significant cost of replacing them if they die. In the parlance of the insurance business, companies have an "insurable interest" in their CEOs that is recognized in law. But buying insurance on the lives of rank-and-file workers is relatively new. Such insurance is known in the business as "janitors insurance" or "dead peasants insurance." Until recently, it was illegal in most states; companies were not considered to have an insurable interest in the lives of their ordinary workers. But during the 1980s, the insurance industry successfully lobbied most state legislatures to relax insurance laws, allowing companies to buy life insurance on the lives of all employees, from the CEO to the mailroom clerk.[5]

By the 1990s, major companies were investing millions in corporate-owned life insurance (COLI) policies, creating what amounted to a multibillion-dollar death futures industry. Among the companies that bought policies on their workers were AT&T, Dow Chemical, Nestlé USA, Pitney Bowes, Procter & Gamble, Walmart, Walt Disney, and the Winn-Dixie supermarket chain. Companies were drawn to this morbid form of investment by favorable tax treatment. As with conventional whole life insurance policies, the death benefits were tax-free, as was the yearly investment income the policies generated.[6]

Few workers were aware that their companies had put a price on their heads. Most states did not require a company to inform employees when it bought insurance on their lives, or to ask workers' permission to do so. And most COLI policies remained in effect even after a worker quit, retired, or was fired. So corporations were able to collect death benefits on employees who died years after leaving the company. Companies kept track of the mortality of their former employees through the Social Security Administration. In some states, companies could even take out life insurance and collect death benefits on the children and spouses of their employees.[7]

Janitors insurance was especially popular among big banks, including Bank of America and JPMorgan Chase. In the late 1990s, some banks explored the idea of going beyond their employees and taking out insurance on the lives of their depositors and credit-card holders.[8]

The booming business in janitors insurance was brought to public attention by a series of articles in *The Wall Street Journal* in 2002. The *Journal* told of a twenty-nine-year-old man who died of AIDS in 1992, yielding a $339,000 death benefit for the company that owned the music store where he had worked briefly. His family received nothing. One article told of a twenty-year-old convenience store clerk in Texas who was shot and killed during a robbery at the store. The company that owned the store offered $60,000 to the young man's widow and child to settle any potential lawsuit, without revealing that it had received a $250,000 insurance payout for the death. The series also reported the grim but little-noticed fact that "after the Sept. 11 terror attacks, some of the first life-insurance payouts went not to the victims' families, but to their employers."[9]

By the early 2000s, COLI policies covered the lives of millions of workers and accounted for 25 to 30 percent of all life insurance sales. In 2006, Congress sought to limit janitors insurance by enacting a law that required employee consent and restricted company-owned insurance to the highest-paid one-third of a firm's workforce. But the practice continued. By 2008, U.S. banks alone held $122 billion in life insurance on their employees. The spread of janitors insurance throughout corporate America had begun to transform the meaning and purpose of life insurance. "It adds up," the *Journal* series concluded, "to a little-known story of how life insurance morphed from a safety net for the bereaved into a strategy of corporate finance."[10]

Should companies be able to profit from the death of their employees? Even some in the insurance industry find the practice distasteful. John H. Biggs, former chairman and CEO of TIAA-CREF, a leading retirement and financial services firm, calls it "a form of insurance that's always seemed revolting to me."[11] But what exactly is wrong with it?

The most obvious objection is a practical one: allowing companies a financial stake in the demise of their employees is hardly conducive to workplace safety. To the contrary, a cash-strapped company with millions of dollars due upon the death of its workers has a perverse incentive to skimp on health and safety measures. Of course, no responsible company would act overtly on this incentive.

Deliberately hastening the deaths of your employees is a crime. Letting companies buy life insurance on their workers does not confer a license to kill them.

But I suspect that those who find janitors insurance "revolting" are pointing to a moral objection beyond the risk that unscrupulous companies might litter the workplace with lethal hazards or avert their eyes from dangers. What is this moral objection, and is it compelling?

It might have to do with the lack of consent. How would you feel if you learned that your employer had taken out a life insurance policy on you, without your knowledge or permission? You might feel used. But would you have grounds for complaint? If the existence of the policy did you no harm, why would your employer have a moral obligation to inform you of it, or to secure your consent?

After all, janitors insurance is a voluntary transaction between two parties—the company that buys the policy (and becomes the beneficiary) and the insurance company that sells it. The worker is not a party to the deal. A spokesman for KeyCorp, a financial services company, put it bluntly: "Employees do not pay premiums, and therefore there's no reason to disclose the details of the policy to them."[12]

Some states don't see it that way and require companies to secure the consent of employees before taking out insurance on them. When companies ask permission, they typically offer workers a modest life insurance benefit as an inducement. Walmart, which took out policies on some 350,000 of its workers in the 1990s, offered a free $5,000 life insurance benefit to those who agreed to be covered. Most workers accepted the offer, unaware of the vast discrepancy between the $5,000 benefit their families would receive and the hundreds of thousands the company would collect upon their deaths.[13]

But lack of consent is not the only moral objection that can be raised against janitors insurance. Even where workers agree to such schemes, something morally distasteful remains. Partly it's the attitude of companies toward workers embodied in such policies. Creating conditions where workers are worth more dead than alive objectifies them; it treats them as commodity futures rather than employees whose value to the company lies in the work they do. A further objection is that COLI policies distort the purpose of life insurance; what was once a source of security for families now becomes a tax break for corporations.[14] It is hard to see why the tax system should encourage companies to invest billions in the mortality of their workers rather than in the production of goods and services.

VIATICALS: YOU BET YOUR LIFE

We can examine these objections by considering another morally complicated use of life insurance that arose in the 1980s and 1990s, prompted by the AIDS epidemic. It was called the viatical industry. It consisted of a market in the life insurance policies of people with AIDS and others who had been diagnosed with a terminal illness. Here is how it worked: Suppose someone with a $100,000 life insurance policy is told by his doctor that he has only a year to live. And suppose he needs money now for medical care, or perhaps simply to live well in the short time he has remaining. An investor offers to buy the policy from the ailing person at a discount, say, $50,000, and takes over payment of the annual premiums. When the original policyholder dies, the investor collects the $100,000.[15]

It seems like a good deal all around. The dying policyholder gains access to the cash he needs, and the investor turns a handsome profit—provided the person dies on schedule. But there's a risk: although the viatical investment guarantees a certain payoff at death ($100,000 in this example), the rate of return depends on how long the person lives. If he dies in one year, as predicted, the investor who paid $50,000 for a $100,000 policy makes a killing, so to speak—a 100 percent annual return (minus the premiums he paid and fees to the broker who arranged the deal). If he lives for two years, the investor must wait twice as long for the same payout, so his annual rate of return is cut in half (not counting additional premium payments, which reduce the return even more). If the patient makes a miraculous recovery and lives for many years, the investor may make nothing.

Of course, all investments carry risk. But with viaticals, the financial risk creates a moral complication not present in most other investments: the investor must hope that the person whose life insurance he buys dies sooner rather than later. The longer the person hangs on, the lower the rate of return.

Needless to say, the viatical industry took pains to deemphasize this ghoulish aspect of its business. Viatical brokers described their mission as providing those with terminal illnesses the resources to live out their last days in relative comfort and dignity. (The word "viatical" comes from the Latin word for "voyage," specifically money and provisions supplied to Roman officials setting out on a journey.) But there is no denying that the investor has a financial interest in the prompt death of the insured. "There have been some phenomenal returns, and there have been some horror stories where people live longer," said William Scott Page, president of a Fort Lauderdale viatical company. "That's sort of the excitement of the viatical settlement. There is no exact science in predicting someone's death."[16]

Some of these "horror stories" led to lawsuits, in which disgruntled investors sued brokers for selling them life insurance policies that failed to "mature" as quickly as expected. The discovery, in the mid-1990s, of anti-HIV drugs that extended the lives of tens of thousands of people with AIDS scrambled the calculations of the viatical industry. An executive of a viatical firm explained the downside of life-extending medication: "A 12-month expectancy turning into 24 months does play havoc with your returns." In 1996, the breakthrough in antiretroviral drugs caused the stock price of Dignity Partners, Inc., a San Francisco viatical company, to plunge from $14.50 to $1.38. The company soon went out of business.[17]

In 1998, *The New York Times* published a story about an irate Michigan investor who, five years earlier, had purchased the life insurance policy of Kendall Morrison, a New Yorker with AIDS who was desperately ill at the time. Thanks to the new drugs, Morrison had returned to stable health, much to the investor's dismay. "I've never felt like anybody wanted me dead before," said Morrison. "They kept sending me these FedExes and calling. It was like, 'Are you still alive?' "[18]

Once an AIDS diagnosis ceased to be a death sentence, viatical companies sought to diversify their business to cancer and other terminal illnesses. Undaunted by the downturn in the AIDS market, William Kelley, executive director of the Viatical Association of America, the industry's trade association, offered an upbeat assessment of the death futures business: "Compared to the number of people with AIDS, the number of people with cancer, severe cardiovascular diseases, and other terminal illnesses is huge."[19]

Unlike janitors insurance, the viatical business serves a clear social good—financing the final days of people with terminal illnesses. Moreover, the consent of the insured is built in from the start (though it's possible that, in some cases, desperately ill people may lack the bargaining power to negotiate a fair price for their insurance policy).

The moral problem with viaticals is not that they lack consent. It's that they are wagers on death that give investors a rooting interest in the prompt passing of the people whose policies they buy.

It might be replied that viaticals are not the only investments that amount to a death bet. The life insurance business also turns our mortality into a commodity. But there's a difference: With life insurance, the company that sells me a policy is betting for me, not against me. The longer I live, the more money it makes. With viaticals, the financial interest is reversed. From the company's point of view, the sooner I die, the better.*

Why should I care if, somewhere, an investor is hoping I die? Perhaps I shouldn't care, provided he doesn't act on his hope or call too often to ask of my condition. Maybe it's merely creepy, not morally objectionable. Or perhaps the moral problem lies not in any tangible harm to me but in the corrosive effect on the character of the investor. Would you want to make a living betting that certain people will die sooner rather than later?

I suspect that even free-market enthusiasts would hesitate to embrace the full implications of the notion that betting against life is just another business. For consider: If the viatical business is morally comparable to life insurance, shouldn't it have the same right to lobby on behalf of its interests? If the insurance industry has the right to lobby for its interest in prolonging life (through mandatory seat belt laws or antismoking policies), shouldn't the viatical industry have

*Life annuities and pensions, which pay out a certain amount each month until death, are more closely analogous to viaticals than is life insurance. The annuity company has a financial interest in the recipients dying sooner rather than later. But annuity risk pools are typically larger and more anonymous than viatical investments, reducing the "rooting interest" in early death. Moreover, annuities are often sold by companies that also sell life insurance, so the longevity risks tend to be offsetting.

the right to lobby for its interest in hastening death (through reduced federal funding for AIDS or cancer research)? As far as I know, the viatical industry did not undertake such lobbying. But if it is morally permissible to invest in the likelihood that AIDS or cancer victims will die sooner rather than later, why isn't it morally legitimate to promote public policies that further that end?

One viatical investor was Warren Chisum, a conservative Texas state legislator and "well-known crusader against homosexuality." He led a successful effort to reinstate criminal penalties for sodomy in Texas, opposed sex education, and voted against programs to help AIDS victims. In 1994, Chisum proudly proclaimed that he had invested $200,000 to buy the life insurance policies of six AIDS victims. "My gamble is that it'll make not less than 17 percent and sometimes considerably better," he told *The Houston Post*. "If they die in one month, you know, they [the investments] do really good."[20]

Some accused the Texas lawmaker of voting for policies from which he stood to profit personally. But this charge was misdirected; his money was following his convictions, not the other way around. This was no classic conflict of interest. It was actually something worse—a morally twisted version of socially conscious investing.

Chisum's brazen glee for the ghoulish side of viaticals was the exception. Few viatical investors were motivated by animus. Most wished good health and long life for people with AIDS—except for the ones in their portfolio.

Viatical investors are not unique in depending on death for their livelihood. Coroners, undertakers, and gravediggers do too, and yet no one morally condemns them. A few years ago, *The New York Times* profiled Mike Thomas, a thirty-four-year-old Detroit man who is the "body retrievalist" for the county morgue. His job is to collect the bodies of people who die and transport them to the morgue. He is paid by the head, so to speak—$14 for each corpse he collects. Thanks to Detroit's high homicide rate, he is able to make about $14,000 per year at this grim work. But when violence wanes, Thomas faces tough times. "I know that's kind of weird to hear," he said. "I mean waiting around for somebody to die. Wishing for someone to die. But that's how it is. That's how I feed my babies."[21]

Paying the corpse collector on commission may be economical, but it carries a moral cost. Giving the worker a financial stake in the death of his fellow human beings is likely to dull his ethical sensibilities—and ours. In this respect, it's like the viatical business but with a morally relevant difference: although the corpse collector depends on death for his living, he need not hope for the early death of any particular person. Any death will do.

DEATH POOLS

A closer analogy to viaticals is death pools, a macabre gambling game that became popular on the Internet in the 1990s, about the same time the viatical industry took off. Death pools are the cyberspace equivalent of traditional office pools on who will win the Super Bowl, except that instead of picking the winner of a football game, players compete to predict which celebrities will die in a given year.[22]

Many websites offer versions of this morbid game, with names such as Ghoul Pool, Dead Pool, and Celebrity Death Pool. One of the most popular is Stiffs.com, which held its first game in 1993 and went online in 1996. For a $15 entry fee, contestants submit a list of celebrities they think are likely to die by year's end. Whoever makes the most correct calls wins the jackpot of $3,000; second place is $500. Stiffs.com attracts more than a thousand participants a year.[23]

Serious players do not make their picks lightly; they scour entertainment magazines and tabloids for news of ailing stars. Current betting favors Zsa Zsa Gabor (age 94), Billy Graham (93), and Fidel Castro (85). Other popular death pool choices are Kirk Douglas, Margaret Thatcher, Nancy Reagan, Muhammad Ali, Ruth Bader Ginsburg, Stephen Hawking, Aretha Franklin, and Ariel Sharon. Since aged and ailing figures dominate the lists, some games award extra points to those who successfully predict long shots like Princess Diana, John Denver, or others who meet untimely deaths.[24]

Death pools predate the Internet. The game has reportedly been popular among Wall Street traders for decades. And Clint Eastwood's last Dirty Harry movie, *The Dead Pool* (1988), involves a death pool that leads to the mysterious murders of celebrities on the list. But the Internet, together with the market mania of the 1990s, brought the ghoulish game to new prominence.[25]

Betting on when celebrities will die is a recreational activity. No one makes a living at it. But death pools raise some of the same moral questions posed by viaticals and janitors insurance. Put aside the Dirty Harry version, in which contestants cheat and try to kill their death pool picks. Is there anything wrong with betting on someone's life and profiting from his or her death? There is something disquieting about it. But provided the gambler doesn't hasten anyone's death, who has a right to complain? Are Zsa Zsa Gabor and Muhammad Ali made worse off when people they've never met place bets on when they'll die? There may be some indignity in rising to the top of the death charts. But the moral tawdriness of the game lies mainly, I think, in the attitude toward death it expresses and promotes.

This attitude is an unwholesome mix of frivolity and obsession—toying with death even while fixating upon it. Death pool participants don't simply place their bets; they partake of a culture. They spend time and energy researching the life expectancy of the people they bet upon. They acquire an unseemly preoccupation with the deaths of celebrities. Death pool websites, replete with news and information about the ailments of well-known figures, encourage this ghoulish fascination. You can even subscribe to a service called Celebrity Death Beeper that sends you an email or text message alert whenever a celebrity dies. Participating in death pools "really changes the way you watch TV and follow the news," says Kelly Bakst, who manages Stiffs.com.[26]

Like viaticals, death pools are morally disquieting because they traffic in morbidity. But unlike viaticals, they serve no socially useful purpose. They are strictly a form of gambling, a source of profit and amusement. Distasteful though they are, death pools are hardly the most grievous moral problem of our time. In the hierarchy of sin, they are boutique vices. But they are interesting for what they reveal, as a limiting case, about the moral fate of insurance in a market-driven age.

Life insurance has always been two things in one: a pooling of risk for mutual security, and a grim wager, a hedge against death. These two aspects coexist in uneasy combination. In the absence of moral norms and legal restraints, the wagering aspect threatens to swamp the social purpose that justifies life insurance in the first place. When the social purpose is lost or obscured, the fragile lines separating insurance, investment, and gambling come undone. Life insurance devolves from an institution to provide security for one's survivors into just another financial product and, finally, into a gamble on death that serves no good beyond the fun and profit of those who play the game. The death pool, frivolous and marginal though it seems, is actually the dark twin of life insurance—the wager without the redeeming social good.

The advent in the 1980s and 1990s of janitors insurance, viaticals, and death pools can be seen as an episode in the commodification of life, and death, in the late twentieth century. The first decade of the twenty-first century carried this tendency farther. But before bringing the story into the present, it's worth looking back to recall the moral unease that life insurance has provoked from the start.

A BRIEF MORAL HISTORY OF LIFE INSURANCE

We commonly think of insurance and gambling as different responses to risk. Insurance is a way of mitigating risk, while gambling is a way of courting it. Insurance is about prudence; gambling is about speculation. But the line between these activities has always been unstable.[27]

Historically, the close connection between insuring lives and betting on them led many to regard life insurance as morally repugnant. Not only did life insurance create an incentive for murder; it wrongly placed a market price on human life. For centuries, life insurance was prohibited in most European countries. "A human life cannot be the object of commerce," a French jurist wrote in the eighteenth century, "and it is disgraceful that death should become a source of commercial speculation." Many European countries had no life insurance companies before the mid-nineteenth century. In Japan, the first one did not appear until 1881. Lacking moral legitimacy, "life insurance did not develop in most countries until the mid- or late nineteenth century."[28]

England was an exception. Beginning in the late seventeenth century, shipowners, brokers, and insurance underwriters gathered at Lloyd's coffeehouse in London, a center of marine insurance. Some came to insure the safe return of their ships and cargo. Others came to bet on lives and events in which they had no stake apart from the wager itself. Many people took out "insurance" on ships they did not own, hoping to profit if a ship was lost at sea. The insurance business commingled with gambling, with the underwriters acting as bookmakers.[29]

English law placed no restrictions on insurance or gambling, which were more or less indistinguishable. In the eighteenth century, insurance "policyholders" placed bets on the outcome of elections, the dissolution of parliament, the chance that two English peers would be killed, the death or capture of Napoleon, and the life of the queen in the months preceding the Queen's Jubilee.[30] Other popular subjects of speculative gambling, the so-called sporting part of insurance, were the outcome of sieges and military campaigns, the "much insured life" of Robert Walpole, and whether King George II would return alive from battle. When Louis XIV, the king of France, fell ill in August 1715, the English ambassador to France wagered that the Sun King would not live beyond September. (The ambassador won his bet.) "Men and women in the public eye usually supplied the subjects for these gaming policies," which amounted to an early version of today's Internet death pools.[31]

One especially grim life insurance wager involved eight hundred German refugees who, in 1765, were brought to England and then abandoned without food or shelter on the outskirts of London. Speculators and underwriters at Lloyd's placed bets on how many of the refugees would die within a week.[32]

Most people would regard such a wager as morally appalling. But from the standpoint of market reasoning, it's not clear what is objectionable about it. Provided the gamblers were not responsible for bringing about the refugees' plight, what's wrong with betting on how soon they will die? Both parties to the bet are made better off by the wager; otherwise, economic reasoning assures us, they wouldn't have made it. The refugees, presumably unaware of the bet, are no worse off as a result of it. This, at least, is the economic logic for an unfettered market in life insurance.

If death bets are objectionable, it must be for reasons that lie beyond market logic, in the dehumanizing attitudes such wagers express. For the gamblers themselves, a cavalier indifference to death and suffering is a mark of bad character. For society as a whole, such attitudes, and the institutions that encourage them, are coarsening and corrupting. As we have seen in other cases of commodification, the corruption or crowding out of moral norms may not, in itself, be adequate grounds for rejecting markets. But since betting on the lives of strangers serves no social good beyond profit and base amusement, the corrupting character of the activity offers a strong reason to rein it in.

The rampant wagering on death in Britain prompted a growing public revulsion against the unsavory practice. And there was a further reason to limit it. Life insurance, increasingly seen as a prudent way for breadwinners to protect their families from destitution, had been morally tainted by its association with gambling. For life insurance to become a morally legitimate business, it had to be disentangled from financial speculation.

This was finally achieved with the enactment of the Assurance Act of 1774 (also called the Gambling Act). The law banned gambling on the lives of strangers and restricted life insurance to those who had an "insurable interest" in the person whose life they were insuring. Since an unfettered life insurance market had led to "a mischievous kind of gaming," parliament now prohibited all insurance on lives "except in cases where the persons insuring shall have an interest in the life or death of the persons insured." "Simply put," writes the historian Geoffrey Clark, "the Gambling Act limited the extent to which human life could be converted into a commodity."[33]

In the United States, the moral legitimacy of life insurance was slow to develop. It was not firmly established until the late nineteenth century. Although a number of insurance companies were formed in the eighteenth century, they sold mostly fire and marine insurance. Life insurance faced "powerful cultural resistance." As Viviana Zelizer writes, "Putting death on the market offended a system of values that upheld the sanctity of life and its incommensurability."[34]

By the 1850s, the life insurance business began to grow, but only by emphasizing its protective purpose and downplaying its commercial aspect: "Until the late nineteenth century, life insurance shunned economic terminology, surrounding itself with religious symbolism and advertising more its moral value than its monetary benefits. Life insurance was marketed as an altruistic, self-denying gift, rather than as a profitable investment."[35]

In time, the purveyors of life insurance became less bashful about touting it as an investment vehicle. As the industry grew, the meaning and purpose of life insurance changed. Once gingerly marketed as a beneficent institution for the protection of widows and children, life insurance became an instrument of saving and investment, and a routine part of business. The definition of "insurable interest" expanded from family members and dependents to include business partners and key employees. Corporations could insure their executives (though not their janitors or rank-and-file employees). By the late nineteenth century, the commercial approach to life insurance "encouraged the insurance of lives for strictly business purposes," extending insurable interest to "strangers linked by nothing but economic interests."[36]

Moral hesitations about commodifying death still hovered in the background. One telling indicator of this hesitation, Zelizer points out, was the need for life insurance agents. Insurance companies discovered early on that people did not buy life insurance on their own initiative. Even as life insurance gained acceptance, "death could not be transformed into a routine commercial transaction." Thus the need for someone to seek out clients, to overcome their instinctive reluctance, and to persuade them of the merits of the product.[37]

The awkwardness of a commercial transaction involving death also explains the low esteem in which insurance salesmen are traditionally held. It's not simply that they work in close proximity to death. Doctors and clergy also do, but they are not tainted by the association. The life insurance agent is stigmatized because he is "a 'salesman' of death, making a profitable living off people's worst tragedy." The stigma persisted in the twentieth century. Despite efforts to professionalize the occupation, life insurance agents could not overcome the distastefulness of treating "death as a business."[38]

The insurable interest requirement limited life insurance to those with a prior stake, whether familial or financial, in the life they were insuring. This helped distinguish life insurance from gambling—no more bets on the lives of strangers simply to make money. But this distinction was not as sturdy as it seemed. The reason: the courts decided that, once you had a life insurance policy (backed by an insurable interest), you could do with it what you pleased, including selling it to someone else. This doctrine of "assignment," as it was called, meant that life insurance was property like any other.[39]

In 1911, the U.S. Supreme Court upheld the right to sell, or "assign," one's life insurance policy. Justice Oliver Wendell Holmes, Jr., writing for the Court, acknowledged the problem: giving people the right to sell their life insurance policies to third parties undermined the insurable-interest requirement. It meant that speculators could reenter the market: "A contract of insurance upon a life in which the insured has no interest is a pure wager that gives the insured a sinister counter-interest in having the life come to an end."[40]

This was precisely the problem that arose, decades later, with viaticals. Recall the insurance policy sold to a third party by Kendall Morrison, the New Yorker with AIDS. For the investor who bought it, the policy was a pure wager on how long Morrison would live. When Morrison refused to die promptly, the investor found himself with a "sinister counter-interest in having the life come to an end." That's what those phone calls and FedEx inquiries were all about.

Holmes conceded that the whole point of requiring an insurable interest was to prevent life insurance from devolving into a death bet, "a mischievous kind of gaming." But this was not reason enough, he thought, to prevent a secondary market in life insurance that would bring the speculators back in. "Life insurance has become in our days one of the best recognized forms of investment and self-compelled saving," he concluded. "So far as reasonable safety permits, it is desirable to give to life policies the ordinary characteristics of property."[41]

A century later, the dilemma that confronted Holmes has deepened. The lines separating insurance, investment, and gambling have all but vanished. The janitors insurance, viaticals, and death pools of the 1990s were only the beginning. Today, markets in life and death have outrun the social purposes and moral norms that once constrained them.

THE TERRORISM FUTURES MARKET

Suppose there were a death pool that did more than entertain. Imagine a website that enabled you to place a bet not on the death of movie stars but on which foreign leaders would be assassinated or overthrown, or on where the next terrorist attack would take place. And suppose the results of this betting pool yielded valuable information that the government could use to protect national security. In 2003, an agency of the Department of Defense proposed such a website. The Pentagon called it the Policy Analysis Market; the media called it the "terrorism futures market."[42]

The website was the brainchild of DARPA (Defense Advanced Research Projects Agency), an agency charged with developing innovative technology for warfare and intelligence gathering. The idea was to let investors buy and sell futures contracts on various scenarios, initially related to the Middle East. Sample scenarios included the following: Would Yasser Arafat, the Palestinian leader, be assassinated? Would King Abdullah II of Jordan be overthrown? Would Israel be the target of a bioterrorist attack? Another sample question was unrelated to the Middle East: Would North Korea launch a nuclear strike?[43]

Since traders would have to back their predictions with their own money, those willing to bet a lot presumably would be the ones with the best information. If futures markets were good at predicting the price of oil, stocks, and soybeans, why not tap their predictive power to anticipate the next terrorist attack?

News of the betting site prompted outrage in Congress. Democrats and Republicans alike denounced the futures market, and the Defense Department quickly canceled it. The firestorm of opposition arose partly from doubt that the scheme would work, but mostly from moral revulsion over the prospect of a government-sponsored betting pool on calamitous events. How could the U.S. government invite people to wager and profit on terrorism and death?[44]

"Can you imagine if another country set up a betting parlor so that people could go in . . . and bet on the assassination of an American political figure?" asked Senator Byron Dorgan (D-ND). Senator Ron Wyden (D-OR) joined Dorgan in demanding the withdrawal of the plan, calling it "repugnant." "The idea of a federal betting parlor on atrocities and terrorism is ridiculous and it's grotesque," Wyden said. Senate Majority Leader Tom Daschle (D-SD) called the program "irresponsible and outrageous," adding, "I cannot believe that anybody would seriously propose that we would trade in death." Senator Barbara Boxer (D-CA) said, "There is something very sick about it."[45]

The Pentagon did not reply to the moral argument. Instead, it issued a statement setting out the principle behind the project, arguing that futures trading had been effective in predicting not only commodity prices but also elections and the box office success of Hollywood movies: "Research indicates that markets are extremely efficient, effective and timely aggregators of dispersed and even hidden information. Futures markets have proven themselves to be good at predicting such things as election results; they are often better than expert opinions."[46]

A number of academics, mainly economists, agreed. One wrote that it was "sad to see poor public relations torpedo a potentially important tool for intelligence analysis." The firestorm of protest had prevented a proper appreciation of the program's merits. "Financial markets are incredibly powerful aggregators of information," two Stanford economists wrote in *The Washington Post*, "and are often better predictors than traditional methods." They cited the Iowa Electronic Market, an online futures market that has predicted the results of some presidential elections better than polls. Another example: orange juice futures. "The futures market in orange juice concentrate is a better predictor of Florida weather than the National Weather Service."[47]

One advantage of prediction markets over traditional intelligence gathering is that markets are not subject to the distortions of information caused by bureaucratic and political pressures. Midlevel experts who know something can go directly to the market and put their money where their convictions are. This could yield information that might be suppressed by higher-ups and never see the light of day. Recall the pressures on the CIA, prior to the Iraq War, to conclude that Saddam Hussein possessed weapons of mass destruction. An independent betting website registered greater skepticism on this question than did CIA Director George Tenet, who declared the existence of such weapons a "slam dunk."[48]

But the case for the terrorism futures website rested on a bigger, broader claim about the power of markets. With market triumphalism at high tide, the defenders of the project articulated a new precept of market faith that had emerged with the age of finance: not only are markets the most efficient mechanisms for producing and allocating goods; they are also the best way of aggregating information and predicting the future. The virtue of DARPA's futures market was that it would "poke, prod and awaken a stubborn intelligence community to the predictive powers of free markets." It would open our eyes "to something that decision theorists have known for decades: The probability of events can be measured in terms of the bets people are willing to make."[49]

The claim that free markets are not only efficient but also clairvoyant is striking. Not all economists subscribe to it. Some argue that futures markets are good at predicting the price of wheat but have a hard time predicting rare events, such as terrorist attacks. Others maintain that, for intelligence gathering, markets of experts work better than ones open to the general public. The DARPA plan was also questioned on more particular grounds: Would it be open to manipulation by terrorists, who might engage in "insider trading" to profit from an attack, or possibly conceal their plans by shorting terrorist futures? And would people really bet on, say, the assassination of the king of Jordan if they knew the U.S. government would use the information to prevent the assassination, thus foiling their wager?[50]

Practicalities aside, what about the moral objection—that a government-sponsored betting pool on death and disaster is repugnant? Suppose the practical difficulties could be overcome, and a terrorism futures market could be designed that would do a better job than traditional intelligence agencies of predicting assassinations and terrorist attacks. Would the moral repugnance of betting and profiting on death and disaster be sufficient reason to reject it?

If the government were proposing to sponsor a celebrity death pool, the answer would be clear: since it achieves no social good, there is nothing to be said for promoting a callous indifference or, worse, a ghoulish fascination with the death and misfortune of others. Betting schemes such as these are bad enough when conducted by private parties. Wanton wagering on death is corrosive of human sympathy and decency, and should be discouraged, not promoted, by the government.

What makes the terrorism futures market morally more complicated is that, unlike death pools, it purports to do good. Assuming it works, it generates valuable intelligence. This makes it analogous to viaticals. The moral dilemma has the same structure in each case: Should we promote a worthwhile end—financing medical needs for a dying person; thwarting a terrorist attack—at the moral cost of giving investors a rooting interest in the death and misfortune of others?

Some say, "Yes, of course." This was the reply of an economist who helped conceive the DARPA project: "In the name of intelligence, people lie, cheat, steal, and kill. Compared to those sorts of things, our proposal was very mild. We were simply going to take money from some people and give it to others based upon who was right."[51]

But this answer is too easy. It ignores the ways that markets crowd out norms. When senators and editorial writers denounced the terrorism futures market as "outrageous," "repugnant," and "grotesque," they were pointing to the moral ugliness of buying a stake in someone's death and hoping that person will die so you can profit. Although there are places in our society where this happens already, having the government sponsor an institution that makes it routine is morally corrupting.

Perhaps, under dire circumstances, this would be a moral price worth paying. Arguments from corruption are not always decisive. But they direct our attention to a moral consideration that market enthusiasts often miss. If we were convinced that a market in terrorist futures was the only way, or the best way, to protect the country from terrorist attack, we might decide to live with the debased moral sensibilities such a market would promote. But that would be a devil's bargain, and it would be important to remain alive to its repugnance.

When markets in death become familiar and routine, the moral opprobrium is not easy to retain. This is important to bear in mind at a time when life insurance is becoming, as it was in eighteenth-century England, an instrument of speculation. Today, betting on the lives of strangers is no longer an isolated parlor game but a major industry.

THE LIVES OF STRANGERS

Life-extending AIDS drugs were a blessing for health but a curse for the viatical industry. Investors found themselves stuck paying premiums on life insurance policies that failed to "mature" as promptly as expected. If the business was to survive, viatical brokers needed to find more reliable deaths to invest in. After looking to cancer patients and others with terminal illnesses, they came up with a bolder idea: Why limit the business to people with diseases? Why not buy life insurance policies from healthy senior citizens willing to cash them in?

Alan Buerger was a pioneer of the new industry. In the early 1990s, he had sold janitors insurance to corporations. When Congress cut back the tax advantages of janitors insurance, Buerger considered moving into viaticals. But then it occurred to him that healthy, wealthy seniors offered a bigger, more promising market. "I felt like I was struck by lightning," Buerger told *The Wall Street Journal*.[52]

In 2000, he began buying life insurance policies from people age sixty-five and older, and selling them to investors. The business works like the viatical business, except that the life expectancies are longer, and the value of the policy is typically higher, usually $1 million or more. Investors buy the policies from people who no longer want them, pay the premiums, and collect the death benefit when the people die. To avoid the taint that came to be associated with viaticals, this new business calls itself the "life settlement" industry. Buerger's company, Coventry First, is one of the most successful in the business.[53]

The life settlement industry presents itself as "a free market for life insurance." Previously, people who no longer wanted or needed their life insurance policies had no choice but to let them lapse, or in some cases to cash them in with the insurance company for a small surrender amount. Now they can get more for their unwanted policies by selling them off to investors.[54]

It sounds like a good deal all around. Seniors get a decent price for their unwanted life insurance policies, and investors reap the benefits when the policies come due. But the secondary market in life insurance has bred a number of controversies and a spate of lawsuits.

One controversy arises from the economics of the insurance industry. Insurance companies don't like life settlements. In setting premiums, they have long assumed that a certain number of people will drop their policies before they die. Once the children are grown and one's spouse is provided for, policyholders often stop paying premiums and let their policies lapse. In fact, almost 40 percent of life insurance policies result in no death benefit payout. But as more policyholders sell their policies to investors, fewer policies will lapse, and the insurance companies will have to pay out more death benefits (i.e., to investors who keep paying the premiums and eventually collect).[55]

Another controversy involves the moral awkwardness of betting against life. With life settlements as with viaticals, the profitability of the investment depends on when the person dies. In 2010, *The Wall Street Journal* reported that Life Partners Holdings, a life settlement company in Texas, had systematically underestimated the life expectancy of the people whose policies they sold to investors. For example, the company sold investors a $2 million insurance policy on the life of a seventy-nine-year-old Idaho rancher, claiming he had only two to four years to live. More than five years later, the rancher, then eighty-four, was still going strong, running on a treadmill, lifting weights, and chopping wood. "I'm healthy as a horse," he said. "There's going to be a lot of disappointed investors."[56]

The *Journal* discovered that the fit rancher was not the only disappointing investment. In 95 percent of the policies Life Partners brokered, the insured person was still alive at the end of the life expectancy the company had predicted. The overly optimistic mortality predictions were made by a doctor in Reno, Nevada, who was employed by the company. Shortly after the article appeared, the company came under investigation for its dubious longevity estimates by the Texas state securities board and the Securities and Exchange Commission.[57]

Another Texas life settlement company was shut down by the state in 2010, for misleading investors about life expectancies. Sharon Brady, a retired law enforcement official in Fort Worth, had been told she could expect a 16 percent annual return by investing in the lives of elderly strangers. "They took out a book and showed us photos and people's ages, and there was a doctor who explained what was wrong with each of them and how long they were supposed to live," Brady said. "You are not supposed to wish someone would die, but you make money if they do. So you are really gambling on when they die."

Brady said she "felt a little strange about it. You get such a high return on the money you put down." It was a disquieting proposition but a financially attractive one. She and her husband invested $50,000, only to learn later that the mortality estimates were, so to speak, too good to be true. "Apparently people were living twice as long as that doctor was telling us."[58]

A further controversial feature of the business involved its inventive ways of finding policies to sell. By the mid-2000s, the secondary market in life insurance had become big business. Hedge funds and financial institutions like Credit Suisse and Deutsche Bank were spending billions buying the life insurance policies of wealthy seniors. As the demand for such policies increased, some brokers began paying elderly people who held no insurance to take out large policies on their lives and then flip the policies to speculators for resale. These policies were called speculator-initiated, or spin-life policies.[59]

In 2006, *The New York Times* estimated that the market in spin-life policies was approaching $13 billion a year. It described the frenzy to recruit new business: "The deals are so lucrative that older people are being wooed in every fathomable way. In Florida, investors have sponsored free cruises for seniors willing to undergo physical exams and apply for life insurance while on board."[60]

In Minnesota, an eighty-two-year-old man bought $120 million worth of life insurance from seven different companies and then sold the policies to speculators at a handsome profit. The insurance companies cried foul, complaining that the purely speculative use of life insurance was at odds with its fundamental purpose of protecting families from financial ruin, and that spin-life policies would drive up the cost of life insurance for legitimate customers.[61]

A number of spin-life policies wound up in court. In some cases, insurance companies refused to pay death benefits, claiming that the speculators lacked an insurable interest. For their part, life settlement companies argued that many insurers, including industry giant AIG (American International Group) had welcomed spin-life insurance business and its high premiums, and complained only when it came time to pay out. Other suits were brought against brokers by the elderly clients they had recruited to buy life insurance for resale to speculators.[62]

One unhappy spin-life client was the TV talk show host Larry King, who had bought and immediately sold two policies on his life, with a total face value of $15 million. King had been paid $1.4 million for his trouble, but he claimed in a lawsuit that the broker had misled him about commissions, fees, and tax implications. King also complained that he could not find out who now held a financial interest in his death. "We don't know whether the owner is a Wall Street hedge fund or a Mafia don," his lawyer said.[63]

The battle between insurance companies and the life settlement industry also played out in state legislatures across the country. In 2007, Goldman Sachs, Credit Suisse, UBS, Bear Stearns, and other banks formed the Institutional Life Markets Association to promote the life settlement industry and to lobby against efforts to restrict it. The association's mission: to create "innovative capital market solutions" for the "longevity and mortality-related marketplace."[64] This was a polite term for the market in death bets.

By 2009, most states had enacted laws banning spin-life, or "stranger-originated life insurance" (STOLI), as it came to be called. But they permitted brokers to continue trading in life insurance policies from ill or elderly people who had bought them on their own, unprompted by speculators. Seeking to fend off further regulation, the life settlement industry sought to draw a principled distinction between "stranger-owned life insurance" (which it supported) and "stranger-originated life insurance" (which it now opposed).[65]

Morally speaking, there's not much difference. For speculators to induce senior citizens to buy and flip life insurance for a quick profit does seem especially tacky. It is certainly at odds with the purpose that justifies life insurance—to protect families and businesses from being financially devastated by the death of a breadwinner or key executive. But all life settlements share this tackiness. Speculating on other people's lives is morally questionable regardless of who originates the policy.

Testifying at a Florida insurance hearing, Doug Head, a spokesman for the life settlement industry, argued that letting people sell their life insurance to speculators "vindicates property rights and represents the triumph of competition and free market economics." Once a person with a legitimate insurable interest buys a policy, he or she should be free to sell it to the highest bidder. "'Stranger owned life insurance' is the natural outgrowth of policy-owners' fundamental property right to sell their policies on the open market." Policies originated or initiated by strangers, Head insisted, are different. They are illegitimate, because the speculator who initiates the policy has no insurable interest.[66]

This argument is unconvincing. In both cases, the speculator who winds up owning the policy has no insurable interest in the elderly person whose death will trigger the payout. A financial stake in the early death of a stranger is created in both cases. If, as Head claimed, I have a fundamental right to buy and sell insurance on my own life, why should it matter whether I exercise this right on my own initiative or at the suggestion of someone else? If the virtue of life settlements is that they "unlock the cash value" of an insurance policy I already own, the virtue of spin-life policies is that they unlock the cash value of my declining years. Either way, a stranger acquires an interest in my death, and I get some money for placing myself in this position.

DEATH BONDS

Only one step remained for the growing market in death bets to come of age—securitization by Wall Street. In 2009, *The New York Times* reported that Wall Street investment banks planned to buy life settlements, package them into bonds, and resell the bonds to pension funds and other big investors. The bonds would generate an income stream from the insurance payouts that came due as the original policyholders died. Wall Street would do for death what, over the past few decades, it had been doing for home mortgages.[67]

According to the *Times*, "Goldman Sachs has developed a tradable index of life settlements, enabling investors to bet on whether people will live longer than expected or die sooner than planned." And Credit Suisse is creating "a financial assembly line to buy large numbers of life insurance policies, package and resell them—just as Wall Street firms did with subprime securities." With $26 trillion of life insurance policies in existence in the United States, and a growing trade in life settlements, the death market offers hope for a new financial product to offset the lost revenue from the collapse of the mortgage securities market.[68]

Although some rating agencies remain to be convinced, at least one believes it is possible to create a bond based on life settlements that minimizes risk. Just as mortgage securities bundle loans from different regions of the country, a bond backed by life settlements could bundle policies on people "with a range of diseases—leukemia, lung cancer, heart disease, breast cancer, diabetes, Alzheimer's." A bond backed by this diversified portfolio of ailments would enable investors to rest easy, because the discovery of a cure for any one disease would not cause the bond price to tank.[69]

AIG, the insurance giant whose complex financial dealings helped bring on the 2008 financial crisis, has also expressed interest. As an insurance company, it has opposed the life settlement industry and fought it in court. But it has quietly bought up $18 billion of the $45 billion in life settlement policies currently on the market and now hopes to package them into securities and sell them as bonds.[70]

What, then, is the moral status of death bonds? In some ways, it is comparable to the death bets that underlie them. If it's morally objectionable to wager on the lives of human beings and to profit from their deaths, then death bonds share this defect with the various practices we've considered—janitors insurance, viaticals, death pools, and all purely speculative trade in life insurance. It might be argued that the anonymity and abstractness of death bonds reduces the corrosive effect on our moral sensibilities to some degree. Once life insurance policies are bundled in vast packages, then sliced and diced and sold off to pension funds and college endowments, no investor retains a rooting interest in the death of any particular person. Admittedly, death bond prices would fall if national health policy, environmental standards, or improved eating and exercise habits led to better health and longer lives. But betting against this possibility seems somehow less troubling than counting the days for the New Yorker with AIDS or the Idaho rancher to die. Or is it?

Sometimes we decide to live with a morally corrosive market practice for the sake of the social good it provides. Life insurance began as a compromise of this kind. To protect families and businesses against the financial risks of an untimely death, societies came reluctantly to the conclusion, over the past two centuries, that those with an insurable interest in a person's life should be permitted to make a wager with death. But the speculative temptation proved difficult to contain.

As today's massive market in life and death attests, the hard-fought effort to disentangle insurance from gambling has come undone. As Wall Street gears up for the death bond trade, we are back to the freewheeling moral universe of Lloyd's coffeehouse in London, only now on a scale that makes their wagers on the death and misfortune of strangers seem quaint by comparison.

5

Naming Rights

Growing up in Minneapolis, I was an avid baseball fan. My team, the Minnesota Twins, played its home games at Metropolitan Stadium. In 1965, when I was twelve years old, the best seats in the park cost $3; bleacher seats were $1.50. The Twins made the World Series that year, and I still have the ticket stub from game seven of the series, which I attended with my father. We sat in the third deck, between home plate and third base. The ticket price: $8. I watched, heartbroken, as the great Dodger pitcher Sandy Koufax defeated the Twins and clinched the championship for the Dodgers.

The star of the Twins in those years was Harmon Killebrew, one of the great home run hitters of all time and now a member of baseball's Hall of Fame. At the peak of his career, he made $120,000 a year. Those were the days before free agency, when teams controlled the right to a player for his entire career. This meant that players had little power to negotiate salaries. They had to play for the team that owned them or not play at all. (This system was overturned in 1975.)[1]

The business of baseball has changed a lot since then. The current star player for the Minnesota Twins, Joe Mauer, recently signed an eight-year contract for $184 million. At $23 million a year, Mauer makes more per game (in fact, more by the seventh inning) than Killebrew made in an entire season.[2]

Not surprisingly, ticket prices have soared. A box seat at a Twins game is now $72, and the cheapest seat in the park costs $11. And Twins' ticket prices are a relative bargain. The New York Yankees charge $260 for a box seat and $12 for an obstructed-view seat in the bleachers. Corporate suites and luxury skyboxes, unheard of in the ballparks of my youth, are even more expensive and generate big revenue for the teams.[3]

Other aspects of the game have changed as well. I'm not thinking here of the designated hitter, the much-debated rule change that spares pitchers from the need to bat in the American League. What I have in mind are changes in baseball that reflect the growing role of markets, commercialism, and economic thinking in contemporary social life. Since its origins in the late nineteenth century, professional baseball has always been a business, at least in part. But in the last three decades, the market mania of the age has left its mark on our national pastime.

AUTOGRAPHS FOR SALE

Consider the sports memorabilia business. Baseball players have long been the object of fervent pursuit by young fans clamoring for autographs. The more obliging players would sign scorecards and baseballs near the dugout before the game, or sometimes after the game as they left the stadium. Today, the innocent autograph scrum has been displaced by a billion-dollar memorabilia business dominated by brokers, wholesalers, and the teams themselves.

My most memorable autograph expedition was in 1968, when I was fifteen. By then, my family had moved from Minneapolis to Los Angeles. That winter, I hung out along the sidelines at a charity golf tournament in La Costa, California. Some of the greatest baseball players of all time were playing in the tournament, and most of them willingly signed autographs between holes. I didn't have the foresight to bring baseballs and indelible Sharpie pens. All I had was a supply of plain three-by-five cards. Some players signed in ink, others with the small pencils they were using to record their golf scores. But I came away with a treasure trove of autographs and the excitement of meeting, however briefly, the heroes of my youth and also some legendary figures who had played before my time: Sandy Koufax, Willie Mays, Mickey Mantle, Joe DiMaggio, Bob Feller, Jackie Robinson, and—yes!—Harmon Killebrew.

It would never have occurred to me to sell these autographs, or even to wonder what they would fetch in the market. I still have them, along with my baseball card collection. But in the 1980s, the autographs and paraphernalia of sports figures came to be viewed as marketable goods and were bought and sold by growing legions of collectors, brokers, and dealers.[4]

Baseball stars began signing autographs for fees that varied with their status. In 1986, Hall of Fame pitcher Bob Feller sold his autograph at collectors' shows for $2 each. Three years later, Joe DiMaggio was signing for $20, Willie Mays for $10 to $12, Ted Williams for $15. (Feller's signing price rose to $10 by the 1990s.) Since these retired baseball greats played in the era before huge salaries, it is hard to fault them for cashing in when the opportunity arose. But active players also joined the signing circuit. Roger Clemens, then a star pitcher for the Boston Red Sox, received $8.50 per autograph. Some players, including Dodgers pitcher Orel Hershiser, found the practice repugnant. Baseball traditionalists bemoaned the paid signings, recalling that Babe Ruth had always signed for free.[5]

But the memorabilia market was only in its infancy. In 1990, *Sports Illustrated* published an article describing how the long-standing practice of autograph seeking was being transformed. The "new breed of autograph collectors" was "rude, relentless and motivated by dollar signs," badgering players in hotels, restaurants, and even in their homes. "While autograph hunters once were simply kids smitten with their heroes, these days the chase also includes collectors, dealers and investors . . . The dealers, often working with paid bands of children—not unlike Fagin and his Artful Dodgers—gather autographs, then turn around and sell them. Investors purchase the autographs on the premise that, like fine art or artifacts of historical importance, a Bird, Jordan, Mattingly or Jose Canseco signature will increase in value over time."[6]

In the 1990s, brokers began paying ballplayers to sign thousands of balls, bats, jerseys, and other items. The dealers then sold the mass-produced memorabilia through catalog companies, cable television channels, and retail stores. In 1992, Mickey Mantle earned a reported $2.75 million to autograph twenty thousand baseballs and make personal appearances, more money than he made during his entire playing career with the Yankees.[7]

But the greatest value attaches to objects that have been used in games. The memorabilia frenzy intensified when, in 1998, Mark McGwire set a new record for most home runs in a season. The fan who caught McGwire's record-setting seventieth home run ball sold it at auction for $3 million, making it the most expensive piece of sports memorabilia ever sold.[8]

The conversion of baseball keepsakes into commodities changed the relation of fans to the game, and to one another. When McGwire hit his sixty-second home run that season, the one that broke the previous record, the person who retrieved the ball did not sell it but promptly gave it to McGwire. "Mr. McGwire, I think I have something that belongs to you," said Tim Forneris, presenting the ball.[9]

Given the market value of the baseball, this act of generosity prompted a torrent of commentary—most of it praising, some critical. The twenty-two-year-old part-time groundskeeper was feted at a Disney World parade, appeared on David Letterman's talk show, and was invited to the White House to meet President Clinton. He spoke in grade schools to children about doing the right thing. Despite these accolades, however, Forneris was chastised for imprudence by a personal finance columnist in *Time*, who described his decision to hand over the ball as an example of "several personal-finance sins that we all commit." Once he "got his mitts on it, the ball was his," the columnist wrote. Giving it to McGwire exemplified "a mind-set that leads many of us into grave errors in daily money matters."[10]

Here then is another example of how markets transform norms. Once a record-setting baseball is seen as a marketable commodity, presenting it to the player who hit it is no longer a simple gesture of decency. It is either a heroic act of generosity or a foolish act of profligacy.

Three years later, Barry Bonds hit seventy-three home runs in a season, breaking McGwire's record. The fight for the seventy-third home run ball led to an ugly scene in the stands and a lengthy legal dispute. The fan who caught it was knocked to the ground by a mob of people trying to grab it. The ball slipped out of his glove and was recovered by another fan standing nearby. Each claimed that the ball was rightfully his. The dispute led to months of legal wrangling and eventually a court trial involving six lawyers and a panel of court-appointed law professors asked to define what constitutes possession of a baseball. The judge ruled that the two claimants should sell the ball and share the proceeds. It sold for $450,000.[11]

Today, the marketing of memorabilia is a routine part of the game. Even the detritus of Major League Baseball games, such as broken bats and used balls, is sold to eager buyers. To assure collectors and investors of the authenticity of game-used gear, every Major League Baseball game now has at least one official "authenticator" on duty. Armed with high-tech hologram stickers, these authenticators record and certify the authenticity of the balls, bats, bases, jerseys, line-up cards, and other paraphernalia destined for the billion-dollar memorabilia market.[12]

In 2011, Derek Jeter's three thousandth hit was a bonanza for the memorabilia industry. In a deal with a collector, the storied Yankee shortstop signed about a thousand commemorative balls, photos, and bats the day after his milestone hit. The autographed balls went for $699.99, the bats for $1,099.99. They even sold the ground on which he walked. After the game in which Jeter collected his three thousandth hit, a groundskeeper gathered five gallons of dirt from the batter's box and shortstop position where Jeter had stood. The bucket containing the sacred earth was sealed and marked with an authenticator's hologram, then sold by the spoonful to fans and collectors. Dirt was also collected and sold when the old Yankee Stadium was torn down. One memorabilia company claims to have sold over $10 million worth of authentic Yankee Stadium dirt.[13]

Some players have sought to cash in on less admirable feats. The all-time hits leader, Pete Rose, who was banished from baseball for gambling on games, has a website that sells memorabilia related to his banishment. For $299, plus shipping and handling, you can buy a baseball autographed by Rose and inscribed with an apology: "I'm sorry I bet on baseball." For $500, Rose will send you an autographed copy of the document banishing him from the game.[14]

Other players have sought to sell even odder items. In 2002, Arizona Diamondbacks outfielder Luis Gonzalez auctioned a piece of used chewing gum for $10,000 online, reportedly for charity. After Seattle Mariners pitcher Jeff Nelson had elbow surgery, he put the bone chips from his elbow up for sale on eBay. The bidding reached $23,600 before eBay halted the auction, citing a rule against the sale of human body parts. (News accounts did not report whether an authenticator was present during the surgery.)[15]

THE NAME OF THE GAME

Players' autographs and paraphernalia are not all that's up for sale. So too are the names of the ballparks. Although some stadiums still bear their historic names—Yankee Stadium, Fenway Park—most major league teams now sell stadium naming rights to the highest bidder. Banks, energy companies, airlines, technology firms, and other corporations are willing to pay hefty sums for the visibility that comes from having their names adorn big-league ballparks and arenas.[16]

For eighty-one years, the Chicago White Sox played in Comiskey Park, named for an early owner of the team. They now play in a commodious stadium called U.S. Cellular Field, named for a mobile phone company. The San Diego Padres play in Petco Park, named for a pet supply company. My old team, the Minnesota Twins, now plays at Target Field, sponsored by the Minneapolis-based retailing giant that also has its name on the nearby basketball arena (the

Target Center) where the Minnesota Timberwolves play. In one of the richest naming rights deals in sports, the financial services firm Citigroup agreed in late 2006 to pay $400 million for a twenty-year right to name the New York Mets' new ballpark Citi Field. By 2009, when the Mets played their first game in the stadium, the financial crisis had cast a cloud over the sponsorship arrangement, which was now being subsidized, critics complained, by the taxpayer bailout of Citigroup.[17]

Football stadiums are also magnets for corporate sponsors. The New England Patriots play in Gillette Stadium, and the Washington Redskins in FedEx Field. Mercedes-Benz recently bought the naming rights to the Superdome in New Orleans, home of the Saints. By 2011, twenty-two of the thirty-two teams in the National Football League played in stadiums named for corporate sponsors.[18]

The selling of stadium naming rights is now so commonplace that it's easy to forget how recently the practice came into vogue. It arose at about the same time that ballplayers began selling their autographs. In 1988, only three sports stadiums had naming rights deals, totaling a mere $25 million. By 2004, there were sixty-six deals, worth a total of $3.6 billion. This accounted for more than half of all the arenas and stadiums in professional baseball, football, basketball, and hockey. By 2010, over one hundred companies had paid to name a big-league stadium or arena in the United States. In 2011, MasterCard bought the naming rights to the former Beijing Olympics basketball arena.[19]

Corporate naming rights do not end with a sign on the stadium gate; increasingly, they extend to the words that broadcasters use in describing the action on the field. When a bank bought the right to name the Arizona Diamondbacks' stadium Bank One Ballpark, the deal also required that the team's broadcasters call each Arizona home run a "Bank One blast." Most teams don't yet have corporate-sponsored home runs. But some have sold naming rights to pitching changes. When the manager heads to the mound to bring in a new pitcher, some broadcasters are contractually obligated to announce the move as an "AT&T call to the bullpen."[20]

Even sliding into home is now a corporate-sponsored event. New York Life Insurance Company has a deal with ten major league baseball teams that triggers a promotional plug every time a player slides safely into a base. So, for example, when the umpire calls a runner safe at home plate, a corporate logo appears on the television screen, and the play-by-play announcer must say, "Safe at home. Safe and secure. New York Life." This is not a commercial message that appears between innings; it is a corporate-sponsored way of announcing the game itself. "This message integrates naturally into the action of the ball game," explains the corporate vice president and advertising director of New York Life. It "is a great reminder to fans who are cheering for their favorite players to reach bases safely, that they too can be safe and secure with the largest mutual life insurance company in the United States."[21]

In 2011, the Hagerstown Suns, a minor league baseball team in Maryland, took commercial sponsorship to the last frontier of the game: they sold the local utility company naming rights to a player's at bats. Each time Bryce Harper, the team's best hitter and major league prospect, came up to bat, the team announced, "Now batting, Bryce Harper, brought to you by Miss Utility, reminding you to call 811 before you dig." What was the point of the incongruous commercial message? Apparently the company believed it was a way to reach baseball fans who worked on construction projects that might damage underground utility lines. The marketing director of the utility company explained: "Addressing the fans before Bryce

Harper digs in at the plate is a great way to remind those in attendance the importance of contacting Miss Utility before every digging project."[22]

So far, no major league team has sold the right to name its players. But in 2004, Major League Baseball did try to sell ads on the bases. In a promotional deal with Columbia Pictures, baseball officials agreed to place a logo for the forthcoming movie *Spider-Man 2* on first, second, and third base at every major league ballpark for three days in June. Home plate would remain pristine. An outpouring of public opposition led to cancellation of the novel product placement. Even in a game cluttered with commercialism, the bases, apparently, are still sacred.[23]

SKYBOXES

Like few other institutions in American life, baseball, football, basketball, and hockey are a source of social glue and civic pride. From Yankee Stadium in New York to Candlestick Park in San Francisco, sports stadiums are the cathedrals of our civil religion, public spaces that gather people from different walks of life in rituals of loss and hope, profanity and prayer.[24]

But professional sports is not only a source of civic identity. It is also a business. And in recent decades, the money in sports has been crowding out the community. It would be an exaggeration to say that naming rights and corporate sponsorships have ruined the experience of rooting for the home team. Still, changing the name of a civic landmark changes its meaning. This is one reason why Detroit fans mourned when Tiger Stadium, named for the team, gave way to Comerica Park, named for a bank. It's why Denver Broncos fans bridled when their beloved Mile High Stadium, which evoked a sense of place, was replaced by Invesco Field, which evokes a mutual fund company.[25]

Of course, sports stadiums are mainly places where people gather to watch athletic events. When fans go the ballpark or arena, they don't go primarily for the sake of a civic experience. They go to see David Ortiz hit a home run in the bottom of the ninth, or to see Tom Brady throw a touchdown pass in the final seconds of the game. But the public character of the setting imparts a civic teaching—that we are all in this together, that for a few hours at least, we share a sense of place and civic pride. As stadiums become less like landmarks and more like billboards, their public character fades. So, perhaps, do the social bonds and civic sentiments they inspire.

The civic teaching of sports is eroded even more powerfully by a trend that has accompanied the rise of corporate naming rights—the proliferation of luxury skyboxes. When I went to see the Minnesota Twins play in the mid-1960s, the difference in price between the most expensive seats and the cheapest ones was $2. In fact, for most of the twentieth century, ballparks were places where corporate executives sat side by side with blue-collar workers, where everyone waited in the same lines to buy hot dogs or beer, and where rich and poor alike got wet if it rained. In the last few decades, however, this has changed. The advent of skybox suites high above the field of play has separated the affluent and the privileged from the common folk in the stands below.

Although luxury boxes first appeared in the futuristic Houston Astrodome in 1965, the skybox trend began when the Dallas Cowboys installed luxury suites at Texas Stadium in the 1970s. Corporations paid hundreds of thousands of dollars to entertain executives and clients in posh settings above the crowd. During the 1980s, more than a dozen teams followed the Cowboys' lead, cosseting well-heeled fans in glass-enclosed perches in the sky. In the late 1980s, Congress cut back on the tax deduction that corporations could claim for skybox expenses, but this did not stem the demand for the climate-controlled retreats.

Revenues from luxury suites were a financial windfall for the teams and drove a stadium construction boom in the 1990s. But critics complained that skyboxes destroyed the class-mixing aspect of sports. "Skyboxes, for all their cozy frivolity," wrote Jonathan Cohn, "speak to an essential flaw in American social life: the elite's eagerness, even desperation, to separate itself from the rest of the crowd . . . Professional sports, once an antidote to status anxiety, have been stricken grievously by the disease." Frank Deford, a writer for *Newsweek*, observed that the most magical element of popular sport was always its "essential democracy . . . The arena made for a grand public convocation, a 20th-century village green where we could all come together in common excitement." But the luxury boxes of recent vintage have "so insulated the swells from hoi polloi that it is fair to say that the American sports palace has come to boast the most stratified seating arrangement in entertainment." A Texas newspaper called skyboxes "the sporting equivalent of gated communities," which enable wealthy occupants "to segregate themselves from the rest of the public."[26]

Despite the complaints, skyboxes are now a familiar feature of most professional sports stadiums, and of many college arenas as well. Although premium seats, including suites and club seats, comprise a small fraction of the total number of seats, they account for almost 40 percent of ticket revenue for some major league teams. The new Yankee Stadium, which opened in 2009, has three thousand fewer seats than its predecessor but three times as many luxury suites. The Boston Red Sox have a waiting list for the forty suites at Fenway Park, which cost up to $350,000 per season.[27]

Universities with big-time sports programs have also found skybox revenues irresistible. By 1996, nearly three dozen university stadiums included luxury boxes. By 2011, almost every major college football program except Notre Dame had them. The federal tax code gives those who use college stadium skyboxes a special tax break, allowing buyers of the luxury suites to deduct 80 percent of the cost as a charitable contribution to the university.[28]

The most recent debate about the ethics of skyboxes took place at the University of Michigan, home of the biggest college stadium in the country. Known as the Big House, Michigan Stadium has attracted more than one hundred thousand fans to every home football game since 1975. When, in 2007, university regents were considering a $226 million renovation plan that included the addition of skyboxes to the iconic stadium, some alumni protested. "One of the great things about college football, especially Michigan football, is that it is a great public space," one alumnus argued, "a place where autoworkers and millionaires can come together to cheer on their team."[29]

A group called Save the Big House gathered petitions in hopes of persuading the regents to reject the luxury suite plan. For 125 years, "the Maize-and-Blue faithful have stood together, shivered together, cheered together and won together, side by side," the critics wrote. "Private luxury boxes represent the very antithesis of that tradition, dividing Michigan fans by income and undermining the unity, excitement and camaraderie that Michigan fans of all ages and backgrounds share as they experience the game together. The very idea of private luxury boxes in Michigan Stadium runs contrary to the egalitarian ideals to which the U-M is dedicated."[30]

The protest failed. The board of regents voted five-to-three to approve the addition of eighty-one luxury suites to Michigan Stadium. When the renovated facility opened in 2010, prices for a suite for sixteen people ranged up to $85,000 per season, parking included.[31]

MONEYBALL

The rise of memorabilia markets, naming rights, and skyboxes in recent decades reflects our market-driven society. A further instance of market thinking in the world of sports is the recent conversion of baseball into "moneyball." The term comes from a 2003 best-selling book by Michael Lewis, who brought insights from the world of finance to bear on a baseball story. In *Moneyball: The Art of Winning an Unfair Game*, Lewis describes how the Oakland Athletics, a small-market team that couldn't afford expensive stars, managed to win as many games as the wealthy New York Yankees, despite having one-third the payroll.

The A's, led by general manager Billy Beane, were able to field a competitive team on the cheap by using statistical analysis to identify players with underappreciated skills and to employ strategies that were at odds with conventional baseball wisdom. For example, they discovered that a high on-base percentage matters more to winning than a high batting average or slugging percentage. So they hired players who, though less celebrated than high-priced sluggers, drew a lot of walks. And despite the traditional view that base stealing wins games, they found that steal attempts generally reduce rather than increase a team's chance of scoring. They therefore discouraged even their speediest players from trying to steal bases.

Beane's strategy succeeded, at least for a time. In 2002, when Lewis followed the team, the Athletics won the western division of the American League. Although they were defeated in the playoffs, the A's story was an appealing David and Goliath tale: an underfinanced, underdog team uses its wits and the tools of modern econometrics to compete with rich, powerhouse teams like the Yankees. It was also, in Lewis's telling, an object lesson in how exploiting market inefficiencies can pay off for shrewd investors. Billy Beane brought to baseball what the new breed of quantitative traders brought to Wall Street—an ability to use computer-driven analysis to gain an edge over old-timers who relied on gut instinct and personal experience.[32]

In 2011, *Moneyball* was made into a Hollywood movie, with Brad Pitt playing the role of Billy Beane. The movie left me cold. At first, I wasn't sure why. Brad Pitt was charming and charismatic as always. So why was the movie so unsatisfying? Partly because it ignored the stars of the team—three excellent young starting pitchers and All-Star shortstop Miguel Tejada—and focused instead on marginal players who had been signed by Beane for their ability to draw walks. But the real reason, I think, is that it's hard to stand up and cheer for the triumph of quantitative methods and more efficient pricing mechanisms. These, more than the players, were the heroes of *Moneyball*.[33]

Actually, I do know at least one person who finds price efficiencies inspiring—my friend and colleague Larry Summers (the economist whose morning prayer about economizing altruism I discussed earlier). In a talk he gave in 2004 while president of Harvard, Summers cited *Moneyball* as illustrative of an "important intellectual revolution that has taken place in the last 30 or 40 years": the rise of social science, and especially economics, "as an actual form of science." He explained how "a very wise baseball general manager hired a Ph.D. in econometrics" to figure out what baseball skills and strategies made for a winning team. Summers glimpsed in Beane's success a larger truth: the moneyball approach to baseball held lessons for the rest of life. "What's true of baseball is actually true of a much wider range of human activity."

Where else, in Summers's view, was the wisdom of the scientific, moneyball approach coming to prevail? In the field of environmental regulation, where "committed activists and attorneys" were giving way to "people who were skilled in performing cost-benefit analyses." In presidential campaigns, where the bright young lawyers who predominated in the past were now less needed than "bright economists and bright MBAs." And on Wall Street, where computer-savvy, quantitative whizzes were displacing schmoozers and inventing complex new derivatives: "In the last 30 years," Summers observed, "the field of investment banking has been transformed from a field that was dominated by people who were good at meeting clients at the 19th hole, to people who were good at solving very difficult mathematical problems that were involved in pricing derivative securities."[34]

Here, just four years before the financial crisis, was the market triumphalist faith—the moneyball faith—on bold display.

As events would show, it didn't turn out well—not for the economy and not for the Oakland Athletics. The A's last made the playoffs in 2006 and haven't had a winning season since. To be fair, this is not because moneyball failed but because it spread. Thanks in part to Lewis's book, other teams, including those with more money, learned the value of signing players with a high on-base percentage. By 2004, such players were no longer a bargain, as rich teams bid up their salaries. The salaries of players who were patient at the plate and drew a lot of walks now reflected their contribution to winning games. The market inefficiencies that Beane had exploited ceased to exist.[35]

Moneyball, it turned out, was not a strategy for underdogs, at least not in the long run. Rich teams could hire statisticians too and outbid poor teams for the ballplayers they recommended. The Boston Red Sox, with one of baseball's biggest payrolls, won World Series championships in 2004 and 2007, under an owner and a general manager who were moneyball apostles. In the years after Lewis's book appeared, money came to matter more, not less, in determining the winning percentage of major league teams.[36]

This is not at odds with what economic theory predicts. If baseball talent is priced efficiently, the teams with the most money to spend on player salaries can be expected to do best. But this begs a bigger question. Moneyball made baseball more efficient, in the economist's sense of the term. But did it make it better? Probably not.

Consider the changes moneyball has wrought in the way the game is played: more protracted at bats, more walks, more pitches thrown, more pitching changes, less free swinging, less daring on the base paths, fewer bunts and stolen bases. It's hard to say this counts as an improvement. A drawn-out at bat with the bases loaded and a tie game in the bottom of the ninth can be a classic baseball moment. But a game littered with long at bats and lots of walks is usually a tedious affair. Moneyball hasn't ruined baseball, but—like other market intrusions of recent years—it's left the game diminished.

This illustrates a point I've tried to make about various goods and activities throughout this book: making markets more efficient is no virtue in itself. The real question is whether introducing this or that market mechanism will improve or impair the good of the game. It's a question worth asking not only of baseball but also of the societies in which we live.

YOUR AD HERE

The world of sports is not the only realm where markets and commercialism run rampant. The last two decades have seen commercial advertising reach beyond its familiar venues—newspapers, magazines, radio, and television—to colonize every corner of life.

In 2000, a Russian rocket emblazoned with a giant Pizza Hut logo carried advertising into outer space. But most of the novel places that ads have been invading since the 1990s are decidedly mundane. In grocery stores, stickers promoting the latest Hollywood movie or network television series began appearing on apples and bananas. Eggs bearing ads for CBS's fall television lineup showed up in the dairy department. The ads were not on the cartons but on each individual egg, thanks to a new laser-etching technology that enabled the company's logo and message to be etched (delicately but indelibly) onto the shell.[37]

Strategically placed video screens enabled advertisers to steal people's attention during the brief moments in the day when even the most harried and distractible have no choice but to stand and wait—in elevators as you wait to reach your floor, at ATMs as you wait for your cash, at gas station pumps as you wait for your tank to fill, even at urinals in restaurants, bars, and other public places.[38]

Restroom advertising used to consist of illicit stickers or graffiti on toilet stalls and restroom walls with phone numbers of prostitutes and escort services. But in the 1990s, it began going mainstream. According to an article in *Advertising Age*, "Marketers like Sony, Unilever and Nintendo along with major liquor companies and TV networks have been elbowing the hookers and cranks aside to get their own commercial messages in front of a demographic with its pants lowered and its zipper undone." Slickly produced ads for deodorants, cars, recording artists, and video games became familiar sights in toilet stalls and on urinal walls. By 2004, bathroom advertising, which targets a young, affluent, and necessarily captive audience, had become a $50 million business. Restroom advertising firms have their own trade association, which recently held its fourteenth annual convention in Las Vegas.[39]

As advertisers began buying space on restroom walls, ads were also finding their way into books. Paid product placement has long been a feature of movies and television programs. But in 2001, the British novelist Fay Weldon wrote a book commissioned by Bulgari, the Italian jewelry company. In exchange for an undisclosed payment, Weldon agreed to mention Bulgari jewelry in the novel at least a dozen times. The book, aptly titled *The Bulgari Connection*, was published by HarperCollins in Britain and Grove/Atlantic in the United States. Weldon more than exceeded the required number of product references, mentioning Bulgari thirty-four times.[40]

Some authors expressed outrage at the idea of a corporate-sponsored novel and urged book editors not to assign Weldon's book for review. One critic said the product placement would likely "erode reader confidence in the authenticity of the narrative." Another pointed to the clunkiness of the product-laden prose as in sentences such as this: "'A Bulgari necklace in the hand is worth two in the bush,' said Doris." Or this: "They snuggled together happily for a bit, all passion spent; and she met him at Bulgari that lunchtime."[41]

Although product placement in books has not become widespread, the emergence of digital reading devices and electronic publishing will likely put the activity of reading books in closer proximity to advertising. In 2011, Amazon began selling two versions of its popular Kindle readers, one with and one without "special offers and sponsored screensavers." The model with special offers costs $40 less than the standard version but comes with rotating ads on the screen saver and at the bottom of the home page.[42]

Flying is another activity that is increasingly suffused with commercialism. We saw in chapter 1 how airlines have turned airport queues into opportunities for profit, by charging extra for access to shorter lines at security checkpoints and for early boarding privileges. But that isn't all. Once you've negotiated the queues, boarded the plane, and settled into your seat, you are now likely to find yourself surrounded by advertisements. A few years ago, US Airways began selling ads on tray tables, napkins, and—improbable though it seems—on airsickness bags. Spirit Airlines and Ryanair, two discount carriers, have slapped ads on the overhead luggage bins. Delta Airlines recently tried showing a commercial for Lincoln cars before the preflight safety video. After complaints that the commercial clutter led passengers to ignore the safety announcement, the airline moved the Lincoln ad to the end of the video.[43]

These days, you don't need to be an author or an airline to attract corporate sponsorship. Simply owning a car will do, provided you are willing to turn your vehicle into a rolling billboard. Ad agencies will pay up to $900 a month to let them wrap your car in a vinyl material bearing logos and product pitches for energy drinks, mobile phone companies, laundry detergents, or the local plumbing supply store. The deals are subject to a few sensible restrictions. If you are advertising a Coca-Cola product, for example, you can't be caught drinking Pepsi while driving. Advertisers estimate that, by driving your ad-draped car around town and in traffic, you will expose as many as seventy thousand people a day to their commercial message.[44]

You can also turn your house into a billboard. In 2011, Adzookie, a small advertising company in California, made an offer of special interest to homeowners facing foreclosure or struggling to make their mortgage payments. If you let the company paint the entire exterior of your house (except the roof) with brightly colored ads, they would pay your mortgage every month for as long as the house displayed the ads. "If you're prepared for the bright colors and stares from neighbors," the company stated on its website, "just complete the submission form below." The company was deluged with interested homeowners. Although it had expected to paint ten homes, the company received twenty-two thousand applications in less than two months.[45]

Even if you lack a car or a house, there is still a way to cash in on the advertising bonanza of recent years: you can make your body a billboard. The practice began, as far as I can tell, at Casa Sanchez, a small, family-owned Mexican restaurant in San Francisco. In 1998, the owners offered a free lunch for life to anyone willing to have the restaurant's logo—a boy in a sombrero riding a giant ear of corn—tattooed on his or her body. The Sanchez family thought that few people, if any, would take them up on the offer. They were wrong. Within months, more than forty people were walking the streets of San Francisco sporting Casa Sanchez tattoos. And often, they'd stop by the restaurant at lunchtime to claim their free burritos.

The owners were pleased with the success of the promotion but sobered when they realized that if everyone with the tattoo showed up for lunch every day for the next fifty years, the restaurant would owe $5.8 million worth of burritos.[46]

A few years later, an ad agency in London began selling advertising space on people's foreheads. Unlike the Casa Sanchez promotion, the tattoos were temporary, not permanent. But the location was more conspicuous. The agency recruited university students willing to wear company logos on their foreheads for £4.20 ($6.83) an hour.

One potential sponsor praised the idea, saying the forehead ads were "an extension of the sandwich board, but a bit more organic."[47]

Other ad agencies developed variations of body advertising. Air New Zealand hired thirty people as "cranial billboards." Participants shaved their heads and wore a temporary tattoo on the back of their heads that read: "Need a Change? Head Down to New Zealand." The payment for displaying the cranial commercial for two weeks: a round-trip ticket to New Zealand (worth $1,200) or $777 in cash (symbolic of the Boeing 777 plane the airline used).[48]

The most extreme body billboard involved a Utah woman, age thirty, who auctioned commercial access to her forehead. As a single mother of an eleven-year-old boy who was struggling in school, Kari Smith needed money for her son's education. In an online auction in 2005, she offered to install a permanent tattoo advertisement on her forehead for a commercial sponsor willing to pay $10,000. An online casino met her price. Although the tattoo artist tried to dissuade her, Smith persisted and had her forehead branded with the casino's website address.[49]

WHAT IS WRONG WITH COMMERCIALISM?

Many people viewed the explosion of naming rights and advertising in the 1990s and early 2000s with distaste, even alarm. The anxiety could be seen in innumerable newspaper headlines: NOWHERE TO RUN, NOWHERE TO HIDE FROM AD BARRAGE (*Los Angeles Times*); AD ONSLAUGHT (*The Sunday Times*, London); ADS INFINITUM (*The Washington Post*); ANYWHERE THE EYE CAN SEE, IT'S NOW LIKELY TO SEE AN AD (*The New York Times*); ADS ARE HERE, THERE, EVERYWHERE (*USA Today*).

Critics and activists decried "tawdry commercial values" and "the debasements of advertising and commercialism." They called commercialism "a pestilence" that was "coarsening hearts, minds, and communities across the country." Some described advertising as "a kind of pollution." A shopper, asked why she disliked finding stickers with movie ads on the fruit in the grocery store, said, "I don't want my apple defiled with advertisements." Even an advertising executive was quoted as saying, "I don't know if anything is sacred anymore."[50]

It is hard to deny the moral force of these concerns. And yet, within the prevailing terms of public discourse, it is not easy to explain what is wrong with the proliferation of advertising we have witnessed in the last two decades.

To be sure, aggressive, intrusive advertising has long been the subject of cultural complaint. Writing in 1914, Walter Lippmann lamented "the deceptive clamor that disfigures the scenery, covers fences, plasters the city, and blinks and winks at you through the night." Ads seemed to be everywhere. The eastern sky was "ablaze with chewing gum, the northern with tooth-brushes and underwear, the western with whiskey, the southern with petticoats, the whole heavens brilliant with monstrously flirtatious women."[51]

Had Lippmann traveled the country roads of the Midwest and the South, his worries would have been confirmed. He would have seen thousands of barns painted in bold colors with advertisements for chewing tobacco: "Chew Mail Pouch Tobacco: Treat Yourself to the Best." Beginning in the late 1890s, the enterprising owners of the Mail Pouch Tobacco Company paid farmers with barns near well-traveled routes $1 to $10 (plus a free paint job) to turn their barns into billboards. These billboard barns, one of the first instances of outdoor advertising, were an early forerunner of the recent attempt to paint ads on people's houses.[52]

Notwithstanding such precedents, the commercialism of the last two decades has displayed a distinctive kind of boundlessness, emblematic of a world in which everything is for sale. Many find such a world unsettling, and rightly so. But what exactly is objectionable about it?

Some say "nothing." Provided the space being sold for ads or corporate sponsorships—the house or barn, the stadium or toilet stall, the biceps or forehead—belongs to the person who sells it, and provided the selling is voluntary, no one has a right to object. If it's my apple or airplane or baseball team, I should be free to sell naming rights and advertising space as I please. This is the case for an unfettered market in advertisements.

As we've seen in other contexts, this laissez-faire argument invites two kinds of objection. One is about coercion and unfairness; the other is about corruption and degradation.

The first objection accepts the principle of freedom of choice but questions whether every instance of market choice is truly voluntary. If a homeowner facing imminent foreclosure agrees to have a garish ad painted on her house, her choice may not really be free but effectively coerced. If a parent, in desperate need of money to buy medicine for his child, agrees to be tattooed to advertise a product, his choice may not be all that voluntary. The coercion objection maintains that market relations can be considered free only when the background conditions under which we buy and sell are fair, only when no one is coerced by dire economic necessity.

Most of our political debates today are conducted in these terms—between those who favor unfettered markets and those who maintain that market choices are free only when they're made on a level playing field, only when the basic terms of social cooperation are fair.

But neither of these positions helps us explain what's troubling about a world in which market thinking and market relationships invade every human activity. To describe what's disquieting about this condition, we need the moral vocabulary of corruption and degradation. And to speak of corruption and degradation is to appeal, implicitly at least, to conceptions of the good life.

Consider the language employed by the critics of commercialism: "debasement," "defilement," "coarsening," "pollution," the loss of the "sacred." This is a spiritually charged language that gestures toward higher ways of living and being. It is not about coercion and unfairness but about the degradation of certain attitudes, practices, and goods. The moral critique of commercialism is an instance of what I've called the corruption objection.

With naming rights and advertising, the corruption can play out on two levels. In some cases, the commercializing of a practice is degrading in itself. So, for example, walking around with a corporate-sponsored tattoo ad on one's forehead is demeaning, even if the choice to sell was freely made.

Or consider this instance of what can only be called extreme naming rights: In 2001, a couple expecting a baby boy put their son's name up for bid on eBay and Yahoo! They were hoping a corporation would buy the naming rights and, in return, provide the loving parents with enough money to buy a comfortable house and other amenities for their growing family. In the end, however, no company met their asking price of $500,000, so they gave up and named their child in the usual way. (They called him Zane.)[53]

Now, you might argue that selling a corporation naming rights to your child is wrong because the child hasn't given his or her consent (the coercion objection). But this isn't the primary reason it's objectionable. After all, children don't usually name themselves. Most of us carry the name our parents gave us, and we don't consider this coercive. The only reason the issue of coercion arises with a corporate-branded child is that going through life with such a name (say, Walmart Wilson or Pepsi Peterson or Jamba Juice Jones) is demeaning—even, arguably, if the child consented to it.

Not all instances of commercialism are corrupting. Some are fitting, like the signage that has long adorned stadium scoreboards, even outfield walls. But it's different when corporate-sponsored banter invades the broadcast booth and asserts itself with every pitching change or slide into second base. This is more like product placement in a novel. If you've listened lately to a baseball broadcast on radio or television, you know what I mean. The unrelenting corporate-sponsored slogans uttered by the announcers intrude upon the game and spoil the inventive, authentic narrative that a play-by-play account of a game can be.

So in order to decide where advertising belongs, and where it doesn't, it is not enough to argue about property rights on the one hand and fairness on the other. We also have to argue about the meaning of social practices and the goods they embody. And we have to ask, in each case, whether commercializing the practice would degrade it.

There is a further consideration: some instances of advertising that are not corrupting in themselves may contribute nonetheless to the commercialization of social life as a whole. Here the analogy to pollution is apt. Emitting carbon dioxide is not wrong in itself; we do it every time we breathe. And yet an excess of carbon emissions can be environmentally destructive. In a similar way, otherwise unobjectionable extensions of advertising into novel settings may, if widespread, bring about a society dominated by corporate sponsorships and consumerism, a society in which everything is "brought to you by" MasterCard or McDonald's. This too is a kind of degradation.

Recall the shopper who didn't want her apples "defiled" by

advertising stickers. Strictly speaking, this is hyperbole. A sticker doesn't defile a piece of fruit (assuming it leaves no bruise). The taste of the apple or banana is unaffected. Bananas have had stickers identifying them as Chiquita for a long time, and few people have complained. Isn't it strange, then, to complain about a sticker promoting a movie or a TV show? Not necessarily. The shopper's objection, presumably, is not to this ad on this apple but to the invasion of everyday life by commercial advertising. The "defilement" is not of the apple but of the common world that we inhabit, increasingly dominated by market values and commercial sensibilities.

The corrosive effect of advertising matters less in the grocery aisle than in the public square, where naming rights and corporate sponsorships are becoming widespread. They call it "municipal marketing," and it threatens to bring commercialism into the heart of civic life. Over the last two decades, financially pressed cities and states have tried to make ends meet by selling advertisers access to public beaches, parks, subways, schools, and cultural landmarks.

MUNICIPAL MARKETING

The trend began in the 1990s. As stadium naming rights deals proved profitable for the owners of major league teams, government officials began seeking corporate sponsorship for municipal services and facilities.

Beach Rescues and Pouring Rights

In the summer of 1998, people arriving for a day at the public beach in Seaside Heights, New Jersey, found five thousand imprints of

Skippy Peanut Butter jars covering the sand for as far as the eye could see. It was the work of a newly invented contraption that can stamp commercials in the sand, and Skippy paid the town a fee to place the beach ads underfoot.[54]

Across the country, in Orange County, California, beach rescues were now brought to you by Chevrolet. In a $2.5 million sponsorship deal, General Motors gave county lifeguards forty-two new pickup trucks and Chevy Blazers with ads proclaiming them the "Official Marine Safety Vehicle of Orange Coast Beaches." The deal also gave Chevrolet free access to the beaches for photo shoots. Ford Rangers were the official beach vehicles for nearby Los Angeles County, where the lifeguards wore swimsuits sponsored by Speedo.[55]

In 1999, Coca-Cola paid $6 million to become the official soft drink of Huntington Beach, California. Under the deal, Coke received exclusive rights to sell its soft drinks, juices, and bottled water at city beaches, parks, and city-owned buildings, along with the use of Huntington Beach's Surf City logo in its advertising.

About a dozen cities across the country had struck similar deals with soft-drink companies. In San Diego, Pepsi won exclusive pouring rights in a $6.7 million deal. San Diego had a number of sponsorship contracts, including one that made Verizon the city's "official wireless partner" and another that made a company called Cardiac Science the city's official supplier of defibrillators.[56]

In New York City, Mayor Michael Bloomberg, a strong proponent of municipal marketing, appointed the city's first chief marketing officer in 2003. His first major initiative was a five-year, $166 million deal with Snapple, which gave the beverage company the exclusive right to sell juices and water in the city's public schools and to sell teas, water, and chocolate drinks in six thousand city-owned buildings. Critics said the Big Apple was selling out to become the Big Snapple. But municipal marketing was becoming a fast-growing business—from only $10 million in 1994 to more than $175 million by 2002.[57]

Subway Stations and Nature Trails

For some public facilities, naming rights deals were slow in coming. In 2001, the Massachusetts Bay Transportation Authority tried to sell naming rights to four historic Boston subway stations, but no corporation was interested. Recently, however, some cities have succeeded in selling naming rights to subway stops. In 2009, New York's Metropolitan Transportation Authority sold Barclays Bank the right to put its name on one of the oldest and busiest subway stations in Brooklyn, for $4 million over twenty years. The London-based bank wanted the naming rights because the station serves a sports arena that also bears the Barclays name. In addition to selling naming rights, the MTA has aggressively sold advertising in the stations, wrapping entire subway trains and blanketing station columns, turnstiles, and floors with ads. Underground ad revenue in the New York subway system increased from $38 million in 1997 to $125 million in 2008.[58]

In 2010, Philadelphia's transportation authority sold AT&T the right to rename Pattison station, a subway stop that had been named for a nineteenth-century Pennsylvania governor. The phone company paid $3.4 million to the authority, plus another $2 million to the advertising agency that arranged the deal. The newly christened AT&T Station is a high-profile location because it serves the stadiums where Philadelphia's sports teams play. The stadiums, by the way, are named for banks and a financial services company: Citizens Bank Park (Phillies baseball), the Wells Fargo Center (76ers basketball and Flyers hockey), and Lincoln Financial Field (Eagles football). A former chair of a citizen advisory committee argued against selling the station's name, observing that "transit is a public service, and names provide an important connection to surrounding streets or neighborhoods." But a transit official replied that the agency needed the money and that selling the name would "help defray costs to customers and taxpayers."[59]

Some cities and states have sought corporate sponsorships for public parks, trails, and wilderness areas. In 2003, the Massachusetts legislature voted to study the feasibility of selling naming rights to the state's six hundred parks, forests, and recreation areas. The *Boston Globe* editorialized that Thoreau's Walden Pond might become "Wal-Mart Pond." Massachusetts did not pursue the plan. But recently, a number of big-name corporate sponsors have struck deals that give their brands a presence in state parks around the country.[60]

North Face, the maker of high-end outdoor apparel, has its logos on trail markers in public parks in Virginia and Maryland. Coca-Cola is allowed to display its logo at a California state park for sponsoring a reforestation project after a wildfire. Nestlé's Juicy Juice brand appears on signs in several New York state parks, where the company installed playgrounds. Odwalla, a rival juice company, funded a tree-planting program in exchange for brand recognition at state parks across the country. In Los Angeles, opponents defeated an attempt, in 2010, to sell advertising in city parks. The promotion would have put ads for a Yogi Bear movie on park buildings, picnic tables, and trash cans.[61]

In 2011, bills were filed in the Florida legislature that would permit the sale of naming rights and commercial advertising along state-owned nature trails. State funding for the greenway system of bicycle, hiking, and canoe trails had been cut in recent years, and some lawmakers saw advertising as a way to compensate for the budgetary shortfall. A company called Government Solutions Group acts as a broker for deals between state parks and corporate sponsors. Shari Boyer, the CEO of the company, points out that state parks are an ideal advertising venue. Those who visit state parks are "excellent consumers," with high incomes, she explains. In addition, the park setting is "a very quiet marketing environment," with few distractions. "It's a great place to reach people; they're in the right state of mind."[62]

Police Cars and Fire Hydrants

In the early 2000s, many cash-strapped cities and towns were tempted by an offer that seemed too good to be true. A company in North Carolina was offering new, fully equipped police cars, complete with flashing lights and backseat jail bars, for $1 per year. The offer came with a small condition: the cars would be covered, NASCAR-style, with ads and commercial logos.[63]

Some police departments and city officials considered the ads a small price to pay for police cruisers that would otherwise cost about $28,000 each. More than 160 municipalities in 28 states signed up for the deal. Government Acquisitions, the company offering the patrol cars, signed contracts with interested towns, then pitched the advertising space to local and national companies. The company insisted the ads would be in good taste—no alcohol, tobacco, firearms, or gaming ads would be accepted. Its website illustrated the concept with a photo of a police car with McDonald's golden arches across the hood. Among the company's clients were Dr Pepper, NAPA Auto Parts, Tabasco hot pepper sauce, the U.S. Postal Service, the U.S. Army, and Valvoline. The company also planned to approach banks, cable television companies, car dealerships, security companies, and radio and television stations as potential advertisers.[64]

The prospect of ad-festooned police cars prompted controversy. Editorial writers and some law enforcement officials opposed the idea, on several grounds. Some worried about the risk of police favoritism toward police car sponsors. Others thought a police department brought to you by McDonald's, Dunkin' Donuts, or the local hardware store demeaned the dignity and authority of law enforcement. Still others argued that the plan reflected badly on government itself and on the willingness of the public to fund essential services. "Some things are so fundamental to the orderly operation of a society," wrote the columnist Leonard Pitts, Jr., "so intrinsic to its dignity, that they have traditionally been entrusted only to people hired and equipped by all of us, collectively, in the interest of the common good. Law enforcement is one of those functions. Or at least, it used to be."[65]

Defenders of the deal acknowledged the awkwardness of having the police hawk commercial products. But in hard financial times, they maintained, the public would rather be served by ad-bearing police cars than by none at all. "People may laugh when they see it going down the road with [commercial] markings on it," said one police chief. "But when that car's responding to an emergency, people are going to be very happy that the car got there." A city councilman in Omaha said he didn't like the idea at first but was swayed by the savings. And he offered an analogy: "Our stadium has ads on the fences and corridors, as does our civic auditorium. As long as it's done tastefully, advertising on police cars is no different."[66]

Stadium naming rights and corporate sponsorships, it turned out, were morally contagious, or at least suggestive. By the time the police car controversy arose, they had prepared the public mind to contemplate further incursions of commercial practices into civic life.

In the end, however, the North Carolina company did not deliver any police cars. In the face of public opposition, including a campaign to dissuade national advertisers from participating, it apparently gave up, and it has since gone out of business. But the idea of advertising on police cars has not disappeared. In Britain, commercially sponsored police cars began to appear in the 1990s, after the Home Office issued new regulations allowing police departments to raise up to 1 percent of their annual budgets from sponsorships. "It's been forbidden territory until recently," a police official said. "Now everything is up for grabs." In 1996, Harrods department store presented special constables in London with a patrol car inscribed in the store's distinctive script: "This car is sponsored by Harrods."[67]

Police car advertising eventually arrived in the United States, though not in NASCAR style. In 2006, the Littleton, Massachusetts, police department introduced a patrol car with three low-key ads for Donelan's Supermarkets, a local grocery store chain. The ads, which look like oversize bumper stickers, appear on the trunk and on each rear fender. In exchange for the publicity, the supermarket pays the town $12,000 per year, which covers the cost of leasing one car.[68]

As far as I know, no one has tried to sell advertising space on fire trucks. But in 2010, Kentucky Fried Chicken entered into a sponsorship deal with the fire department of Indianapolis to promote the launch of a new menu item—"fiery" grilled chicken wings. The deal included a photo shoot with the Indianapolis fire department and the placing of KFC logos (including the iconic image of Colonel Sanders) on fire extinguishers at city recreation centers. In another Indiana town, KFC paid for a similar promotion in exchange for the right to put KFC logos on fire hydrants.[69]

Jails and Schools

Advertising has also invaded the two institutions most central to civil authority and public purpose: jails and schools. In 2011, the Erie County Holding Center in Buffalo, New York, began running ads on a high-definition television screen that defendants see moments after their arrest. What advertisers would want to reach this audience? Bail bondsmen and defense lawyers. The commercials sell for $40 per week with a one-year commitment. They run along with information from the holding center about rules and visiting hours. The ads also appear on a screen in a lobby used by family and friends waiting to visit the inmates. The county government receives a third of the advertising revenue, which will boost county coffers by $8,000 to $15,000 a year.[70]

The ads sold out quickly. Anthony N. Diina, the head of the ad company that set up the arrangement, explained its appeal: "What do people want when they are in the Holding Center? They want to get out. And they don't want to get convicted. So they want bail. And an attorney." The ads and the audience were a perfect fit. "You want to advertise to someone exactly when they want to make their decision," Diina told *The Buffalo News*. "That is the case here. This is the ultimate captive audience."[71]

Channel One streams advertising messages to a captive audience of a different kind: the millions of teenagers required to watch it in classrooms across the country. The commercial-sponsored twelve-minute television news program was launched in 1989 by Chris Whittle, an entrepreneur. Whittle offered schools free television sets, video equipment, and a satellite link in exchange for an agreement to show the program every day and to require students to watch it, including the two minutes of commercials it contained. Although New

York State banned Channel One from its schools, most states did not, and by 2000, Channel One was seen by eight million students in twelve thousand schools. Since it reached more than 40 percent of the nation's teenagers, it was able to charge advertisers such as Pepsi, Snickers, Clearasil, Gatorade, Reebok, Taco Bell, and the U.S. Army premium rates, about $200,000 per thirty-second spot (comparable to ad rates on network television).[72]

A Channel One executive explained its financial success at a youth marketing conference in 1994: "The biggest selling point to advertisers [is that] we are forcing kids to watch two minutes of commercials. The advertiser gets a group of kids who cannot go to the bathroom, who cannot change the station, who cannot listen to their mother yell in the background, who cannot be playing Nintendo, who cannot have their headsets on."[73]

Whittle sold Channel One some years ago and is now starting a for-profit private school in New York. His former company is no longer the potent force it once was. Since its peak in the early 2000s, Channel One has lost about a third of its schools and many of its major advertisers. But it succeeded in shattering the taboo against commercials in the classroom. Today, public schools are awash in advertising, corporate sponsorships, product placement, even naming rights.[74]

The presence of commercialism in classrooms is not altogether new. In the 1920s, Ivory Soap donated bars of Ivory to schools for soap-carving competitions. The placing of company logos on scoreboards and ads in high school yearbooks has long been a common practice. But the 1990s brought a dramatic increase in corporate involvement in schools. Companies flooded teachers with free videos, posters, and "learning kits" designed to burnish corporate images and emblazon brand names in the minds of children. They called them "sponsored educational materials." Students could learn about nutrition from curricular materials supplied by Hershey's Chocolate or McDonald's, or study the effects of an Alaska oil spill in a video made by Exxon. Procter & Gamble offered an environmental curriculum that explained why disposable diapers were good for the earth.[75]

In 2009, Scholastic, the world's largest publisher of children's books, distributed free curricular materials about the energy industry to sixty-six thousand fourth-grade teachers. The curriculum, called the "United States of Energy," was funded by the American Coal Foundation. The industry-sponsored lesson plan highlighted the benefits of coal but made no mention of mining accidents, toxic waste, greenhouse gases, or other environmental effects. When press accounts reported widespread criticism of the one-sided curriculum, Scholastic announced that it would scale back its corporate-sponsored publications.[76]

Not all corporate-sponsored freebies promote ideological agendas. Some simply plug the brand. In one well-known example, the Campbell Soup Company sent out a free science kit that purported to teach the scientific method. With the use of a slotted spoon (included in the kit), students were shown how to prove that Campbell's Prego spaghetti sauce was thicker than Ragú, the rival brand. General Mills sent teachers a science curriculum on volcanoes called "Gushers: Wonders of the Earth." The kit included free samples of its Fruit Gushers candy, with soft centers that "gushed" when bitten. The teacher's guide suggested that students bite into the Gushers and compare the effect to a geothermal eruption. A Tootsie Roll kit showed how third graders could practice math by counting Tootsie Rolls. For a writing assignment, it recommended that children interview family members about their memories of Tootsie Rolls.[77]

The surge in advertising in schools reflects the increased buying power of children and their growing influence on family spending. In 1983, U.S. companies spent $100 million advertising to children. In 2005, they spent $16.8 billion. Since children are in school most of the day, marketers work aggressively to reach them there. Meanwhile, inadequate funding for education has made public schools only too willing to welcome them.[78]

In 2001, an elementary school in New Jersey became the nation's first public school to sell naming rights to a corporate sponsor. In exchange for a $100,000 donation from a local supermarket, it renamed its gym the ShopRite of Brooklawn Center. Other naming rights deals followed. The most lucrative were for high school football fields, ranging from $100,000 to $1 million. In 2006, a new public high school in Philadelphia aimed high. It announced a price list of available naming rights: $1 million for the performing arts pavilion, $750,000 for the gym, $50,000 for the science labs, and $5 million to name the school itself. Microsoft gave $100,000 to name the school's visitors center. Some naming opportunities are less expensive. A high school in Newburyport, Massachusetts, offered naming rights to the principal's office for $10,000.[79]

Many school districts have gone for straight-out advertising—in every conceivable space. In 2011, a Colorado school district sold advertising space on report cards. A few years earlier, a Florida elementary school issued report cards in jackets bearing a promotion for McDonald's, including a cartoon of Ronald McDonald and the Golden Arches logo. The ad was actually part of a "report card incentive" scheme that offered children with all A's and B's, or with fewer than three absences, a free Happy Meal at McDonald's. Local opposition led to cancellation of the promotion.[80]

By 2011, seven states had approved advertising on the sides of school buses. School bus ads began in the 1990s in Colorado, whose schools were also among the first to accept advertising indoors. In Colorado Springs, ads for Mountain Dew adorned school hallways, and ads for Burger King decorated the sides of school buses. More recently, schools in Minnesota, Pennsylvania, and elsewhere have allowed advertisers to install massive "supergraphic" ads on walls and floors, shrink-wrapped over lockers, locker-room benches, and cafeteria tables.[81]

The rampant commercialization of schools is corrupting in two ways. First, most corporate-sponsored curricular material is ridden with bias, distortion, and superficial fare. A study by Consumers Union found, not surprisingly, that nearly 80 percent of sponsored educational materials are slanted toward the sponsor's product or point of view. But even if corporate sponsors supplied objective teaching tools of impeccable quality, commercial advertising would still be a pernicious presence in the classroom, because it is at odds with the purpose of schools. Advertising encourages people to want things and to satisfy their desires. Education encourages people to reflect critically on their desires, to restrain or to elevate them. The purpose of advertising is to recruit consumers; the purpose of public schools is to cultivate citizens.[82]

It isn't easy to teach students to be citizens, capable of thinking critically about the world around them, when so much of childhood consists of basic training for a consumer society. At a time when many children come to school as walking billboards of logos and labels and licensed apparel, it is all the more difficult—and all the more important—for schools to create some distance from a popular culture steeped in the ethos of consumerism.

But advertising abhors distance. It blurs the boundaries between places and makes every setting a site for selling. "Discover your own river of revenue at the schoolhouse gates!" proclaimed a brochure promoting a marketing conference for school advertisers. "Whether it's first-graders learning to read or teenagers shopping for their first car, we can guarantee an introduction of your product and your company to these students in the traditional setting of the classroom!"[83]

As the marketers storm the schoolhouse gates, cash-strapped schools, reeling from recession, property tax caps, budget cuts, and rising enrollments, feel no choice but to let them in. But the fault lies less in our schools than in us citizens. Rather than raise the public funds we need to educate our children, we choose instead to sell their time and rent their minds to Burger King and Mountain Dew.

SKYBOXIFICATION

Commercialism does not destroy everything it touches. A fire hydrant with a KFC logo still delivers water to douse the flames. A subway car shrink-wrapped in ads for a Hollywood movie can still get you home in time for dinner. Children can learn arithmetic by counting Tootsie Rolls. Sports fans still root for the home team in Bank of America Stadium, AT&T Park, and Lincoln Financial Field, even if few of us can name the teams that call those places home.

Nevertheless, imprinting things with corporate logos changes their meaning. Markets leave their mark. Product placement spoils the integrity of books and corrupts the relationship of author and reader. Tattooed body ads objectify and demean the people paid to wear them. Commercials in classrooms undermine the educational purpose of schools.

These are, I admit, contestable judgments. People disagree about the meaning of books, bodies, and schools, and how they should be valued. In fact, we disagree about the norms appropriate to many of the domains that markets have invaded—family life, friendship, sex, procreation, health, education, nature, art, citizenship, sports, and the way we contend with the prospect of death. But that's my point: once we see that markets and commerce change the character of the goods they touch, we have to ask where markets belong—and where they don't. And we can't answer this question without deliberating about the meaning and purpose of goods, and the values that should govern them.

Such deliberations touch, unavoidably, on competing conceptions of the good life. This is terrain on which we sometimes fear to tread. For fear of disagreement, we hesitate to bring our moral and spiritual convictions into the public square. But shrinking from these questions does not leave then undecided. It simply means that markets will decide them for us. This is the lesson of the last three decades. The era of market triumphalism has coincided with a time when public discourse has been largely empty of moral and spiritual substance. Our only hope of keeping markets in their place is to deliberate openly and publicly about the meaning of the goods and social practices we prize.

In addition to debating the meaning of this or that good, we also need to ask a bigger question, about the kind of society in which we wish to live. As naming rights and municipal marketing appropriate the common world, they diminish its public character. Beyond the damage it does to particular goods, commercialism erodes commonality. The more things money can buy, the fewer the occasions when people from different walks of life encounter one another. We see this when we go to a baseball game and gaze up at the skyboxes, or down from them, as the case may be. The disappearance of the class-mixing experience once found at the ballpark represents a loss not only for those looking up but also for those looking down.

Something similar has been happening throughout our society. At a time of rising inequality, the marketization of everything means that people of affluence and people of modest means lead increasingly separate lives. We live and work and shop and play in different places. Our children go to different schools. You might call it the skyboxification of American life. It's not good for democracy, nor is it a satisfying way to live.

Democracy does not require perfect equality, but it does require that citizens share in a common life. What matters is that people of different backgrounds and social positions encounter one another, and bump up against one another, in the course of everyday life. For this is how we learn to negotiate and abide our differences, and how we come to care for the common good.

And so, in the end, the question of markets is really a question about how we want to live together. Do we want a society where everything is up for sale? Or are there certain moral and civic goods that markets do not honor and money cannot buy?

Notes

Acknowledgments

Index

Notes

Introduction: Markets and Morals

1. Jennifer Steinhauer, "For $82 a Day, Booking a Cell in a 5-Star Jail," *New York Times*, April 29, 2007.
2. Daniel Machalaba, "Paying for VIP Treatment in a Traffic Jam: More Cities Give Drivers Access to Express Lanes—for a Fee," *Wall Street Journal*, June 21, 2007.
3. Sam Dolnick, "World Outsources Pregnancies to India," *USA Today*, December 31, 2007; Amelia Gentleman, "India Nurtures Business of Surrogate Motherhood," *New York Times*, March 10, 2008.
4. Eliot Brown, "Help Fund a Project, and Get a Green Card," *Wall Street Journal*, February 2, 2011; Sumathi Reddy, "Program Gives Investors Chance at Visa," *Wall Street Journal*, June 7, 2011.
5. Brendan Borrell, "Saving the Rhino Through Sacrifice," *Bloomberg Businessweek*, December 9, 2010.
6. Tom Murphy, "Patients Paying for Extra Time with Doctor: 'Concierge' Practices, Growing in Popularity, Raise Access Concerns," *Washington Post*, January 24, 2010; Paul Sullivan, "Putting Your Doctor, or a Whole Team of Them, on Retainer," *New York Times*, April 30, 2011.
7. The current price in euros can be found at www.pointcarbon.com.
8. Daniel Golden, "At Many Colleges, the Rich Kids Get Affirmative Action: Seeking Donors, Duke Courts 'Development Admits,'" *Wall Street Journal*, February 20, 2003.
9. Andrew Adam Newman, "The Body as Billboard: Your Ad Here," *New York Times*, February 18, 2009.
10. Carl Elliott, "Guinea-Pigging," *New Yorker*, January 7, 2008.

11. Matthew Quirk, "Private Military Contractors: A Buyer's Guide," *Atlantic*, September 2004, p. 39, quoting P. W. Singer; Mark Hemingway, "Warriors for Hire," *Weekly Standard*, December 18, 2006; Jeffrey Gettleman, Mark Massetti, and Eric Schmitt, "U.S. Relies on Contractors in Somalia Conflict," *New York Times*, August 10, 2011.
12. Sarah O'Connor, "Packed Agenda Proves Boon for Army Standing in Line," *Financial Times*, October 13, 2009; Lisa Lerer, "Waiting for Good Dough," *Politico*, July 26, 2007; Tara Palmeri, "Homeless Stand in for Lobbyists on Capitol Hill," CNN, http://edition.cnn.com/2009/POLITICS/07/13/line.standers/.
13. Amanda Ripley, "Is Cash the Answer?" *Time*, April 19, 2010, pp. 44–45.
14. In one weight-loss study, participants earned an average of $378.49 for losing fourteen pounds over sixteen weeks. See Kevin G. Volpp, "Paying People to Lose Weight and Stop Smoking," *Issue Brief*, Leonard Davis Institute of Health Economics, University of Pennsylvania, vol. 14, February 2009; K. G. Volpp et al., "Financial Incentive–Based Approaches for Weight Loss," *JAMA* 300 (December 10, 2008): 2631–37.
15. Sophia Grene, "Securitising Life Policies Has Dangers," *Financial Times*, August 2, 2010; Mark Maremont and Leslie Scism, "Odds Skew Against Investors in Bets on Strangers' Lives," *Wall Street Journal*, December 21, 2010.
16. T. Christian Miller, "Contractors Outnumber Troops in Iraq," *Los Angeles Times*, July 4, 2007; James Glanz, "Contractors Outnumber U.S. Troops in Afghanistan," *New York Times*, September 2, 2009.
17. "Policing for Profit: Welcome to the New World of Private Security," *Economist*, April 19, 1997.
18. I am indebted here to Elizabeth Anderson's illuminating account in *Value in Ethics and Economics* (Cambridge, MA: Harvard University Press, 1993).
19. Edmund L. Andrews, "Greenspan Concedes Error on Regulation," *New York Times*, October 24, 2008.
20. "What Went Wrong with Economics," *The Economist*, July 16, 2009.
21. Frank Newport, "Americans Blame Government More Than Wall Street for Economy," Gallup Poll, October 19, 2011, www.gallup.com/poll/150191/Americans-Blame-Gov-Wall-Street-Economy.aspx.
22. William Douglas, "Occupy Wall Street Shares Roots with Tea Party Protesters—but Different Goals," *Miami Herald*, October 19, 2011; David S. Meyer, "What Occupy Wall Street Learned from the Tea Party," *Washington Post*, October 7, 2011; Dunstan Prial, "Occupy Wall Street, Tea Party Movements Both Born of Bank Bailouts," Fox Business, October 20, 2011, www.foxbusiness.com/markets/2011/10/19/occupy-wall-street-tea-party-born-bank-bailouts.

1. *Jumping the Queue*

1. Christopher Caldwell, "First-Class Privilege," *New York Times Magazine*, May 11, 2008, pp. 9–10.
2. The United Airlines Premier Line is described at https://store.united.com/traveloptions/control/category?category_id=UM_PMRLINE&navSource=Travel+Options+Main+Menu&linkTitle=UM_PMRLINE; David Millward, "Luton Airport Charges to Jump Security Queue," *Telegraph*, March 26, 2009, www.london-luton.co.uk/en/prioritylane.
3. Caldwell, "First-Class Privilege."
4. Ramin Setoodeh, "Step Right Up! Amusement-Park Visitors Pay Premium to Avoid Long Lines," *Wall Street Journal*, July 12, 2004, p. B1; Chris Mohney, "Changing Lines: Paying to Skip the Queues at Theme Parks," Slate, July 3, 2002; Steve Rushin, "The Waiting Game," *Time*, September 10, 2007, p. 88; Harry Wallop, "£350 to Queue Jump at a Theme Park," *Telegraph*, February 13, 2011. The quote is from Mohney, "Changing Lines."
5. Setoodeh, "Step Right Up!"; Mohney, "Changing Lines"; www.universalstudioshollywood.com/ticket_front_of_line.html.
6. www.esbnyc.com/observatory_visitors_tips.asp; https://ticketing.esbnyc.com/Webstore/Content.aspx?Kind=LandingPage.
7. www.hbo.com/curb-your-enthusiasm/episodes/index.html#1/curb-your-enthusiasm/episodes/4/36-the-car-pool-lane/synopsis.html.
8. Timothy Egan, "Paying on the Highway to Get Out of First Gear," *New York Times*, April 28, 2005, p. A1; Larry Copeland, "Solo in the Car-pool Lane?" *USA Today*, May 9, 2005, p. 3A; Daniel Machalaba, "Paying for VIP Treatment in a Traffic Jam," *Wall Street Journal*, June 21, 2007, p. 1; Larry Lane, "'HOT' Lanes Wide Open to Solo Drivers—For a Price," *Seattle Post-Intelligencer*, April 3, 2008, p. A1; Michael Cabanatuan, "Bay Area's First Express Lane to Open on I-680," *San Francisco Chronicle*, September 13, 2010.
9. Joe Dziemianowicz, "Shakedown in the Park: Putting a Price on Free Shakespeare Tickets Sparks an Ugly Drama," *Daily News*, June 9, 2010, p. 39.
10. Ibid.; Glenn Blain, "Attorney General Andrew Cuomo Cracks Down on Scalping of Shakespeare in the Park Tickets," *Daily News*, June 11, 2010; "Still Acting Like Attorney General, Cuomo Goes After Shakespeare Scalpers," *Wall Street Journal*, June 11, 2010.
11. Brian Montopoli, "The Queue Crew," *Legal Affairs*, January/February 2004; Libby Copeland, "The Line Starts Here," *Washington Post*, March 2, 2005; Lisa Lerer, "Waiting for Good Dough," *Politico*, July 26, 2007; Tara Palmeri, "Homeless

Stand in for Lobbyists on Capitol Hill," CNN, http://edition.cnn.com/2009/POLITICS/07/13/line.standers.

12. Sam Hananel, "Lawmaker Wants to Ban Hill Line Standers," *Washington Post*, October 17, 2007; Mike Mills, "It Pays to Wait: On the Hill, Entrepreneurs Take Profitable Queue from Lobbyists," *Washington Post*, May 24, 1995; "Hustling Congress," *Washington Post*, May 29, 1995. Senator McCaskill is quoted in Sarah O'Connor, "Packed Agenda Proves Boon for Army Standing in Line," *Financial Times*, October 13, 2009.
13. Robyn Hagan Cain, "Need a Seat at Supreme Court Oral Arguments? Hire a Line Stander," FindLaw, September 2, 2011, http://blogs.findlaw.com/supreme_court/2011/09/need-a-seat-at-supreme-court-oral-arguments-hire-a-line-stander.html; www.qmsdc.com/linestanding.html.
14. www.linestanding.com. Statement by Mark Gross at http://qmsdc.com/Response%20to%20S-2177.htm.
15. Gomes quoted in Palmeri, "Homeless Stand in for Lobbyists on Capitol Hill."
16. Ibid.
17. David Pierson, "In China, Shift to Privatized Healthcare Brings Long Lines and Frustration," *Los Angeles Times*, February 11, 2010; Evan Osnos, "In China, Health Care Is Scalpers, Lines, Debt," *Chicago Tribune*, September 28, 2005; "China Focus: Private Hospitals Shoulder Hopes of Revamping China's Ailing Medical System," Xinhua News Agency, March 11, 2010, www.istockanalyst.com/article/viewiStockNews/articleid/3938009.
18. Yang Wanli, "Scalpers Sell Appointments for 3,000 Yuan," *China Daily*, December 24, 2009, www.chinadaily.com.cn/bizchina/2009-12/24/content_9224785.htm; Pierson, "In China, Shift to Privatized Healthcare Brings Long Lines and Frustration."
19. Osnos, "In China, Health Care Is Scalpers, Lines, Debt."
20. Murphy, "Patients Paying for Extra Time with Doctor"; Abigail Zuger, "For a Retainer, Lavish Care by 'Boutique Doctors,'" *New York Times*, October 30, 2005.
21. Paul Sullivan, "Putting Your Doctor, or a Whole Team of Them, on Retainer," *New York Times*, April 30, 2011, p. 6; Kevin Sack, "Despite Recession, Personalized Health Care Remains in Demand," *New York Times*, May 11, 2009.
22. Sack, "Despite Recession, Personalized Health Care Remains in Demand."
23. www.md2.com/md2-vip-medical.php.
24. www.md2.com/md2-vip-medical.php?qsx=21.
25. Samantha Marshall, "Concierge Medicine," *Town & Country*, January 2011.
26. Sullivan, "Putting Your Doctor, or a Whole Team of Them, on Retainer"; Drew Lindsay, "I Want to Talk to My Doctor," *Washingtonian*, February 2010, pp. 27–33.

27. Zuger, "For a Retainer, Lavish Care by 'Boutique Doctors.'"
28. Lindsay, "I Want to Talk to My Doctor"; Murphy, "Patients Paying for Extra Time with Doctor"; Zuger, "For a Retainer, Lavish Care by 'Boutique Doctors'"; Sack, "Despite Recession, Personalized Health Care Remains in Demand."
29. A recent study found that, in Massachusetts, the majority of family physicians and internal medicine physicians were not accepting new patients. See Robert Pear, "U.S. Plans Stealth Survey on Access to Doctors," *New York Times*, June 26, 2011.
30. N. Gregory Mankiw, *Principles of Microeconomics*, 5th ed. (Mason, OH: South-Western Cengage Learning, 2009), pp. 147, 149, 151.
31. N. Gregory Mankiw, *Principles of Microeconomics*, 1st ed. (Mason, OH: South-Western Cengage Learning, 1998), p. 148.
32. Blain, "Attorney General Cuomo Cracks Down on Scalping of Shakespeare in the Park Tickets."
33. Richard H. Thaler, an economist, quoted in John Tierney, "Tickets? Supply Meets Demand on Sidewalk," *New York Times*, December 26, 1992.
34. Marjie Lundstrom, "Scalpers Flipping Yosemite Reservations," *Sacramento Bee*, April 18, 2011.
35. "Scalpers Strike Yosemite Park: Is Nothing Sacred?" editorial, *Sacramento Bee*, April 19, 2011.
36. Suzanne Sataline, "In First U.S. Visit, Pope Benedict Has Mass Appeal: Catholic Church Tries to Deter Ticket Scalping," *Wall Street Journal*, April 16, 2008.
37. John Seabrook, "The Price of the Ticket," *New Yorker*, August 10, 2009. The $4 million figure comes from Marie Connolly and Alan B. Kreuger, "Rockonomics: The Economics of Popular Music," March 2005, working paper, www.krueger.princeton.edu/working_papers.html.
38. Seabrook, "The Price of the Ticket."
39. Andrew Bibby, "Big Spenders Jump the Queue," *Mail on Sunday* (London), March 13, 2006; Steve Huettel, "Delta Thinks of Charging More for American Voice on the Phone," *St. Petersburg Times*, July 28, 2004; Gersh Kuntzman, "Delta Nixes Special Fee for Tickets," *New York Post*, July 29, 2004.

2. Incentives

1. Michelle Cottle, "Say Yes to CRACK," *New Republic*, August 23, 1999; William Lee Adams, "Why Drug Addicts Are Getting Sterilized for Cash," *Time*, April 17, 2010. The number of addicts and alcoholics (including women and men) accepting payment for sterilization or long-term contraception from Project Prevention, as of August 2011, was 3,848, according to http://projectprevention.org/statistics.

2. Pam Belluck, "Cash for Sterilization Plan Draws Addicts and Critics," *New York Times*, July 24, 1999; Adams, "Why Drug Addicts Are Getting Sterilized for Cash"; Cottle, "Say Yes to CRACK."
3. Adams, "Why Drug Addicts Are Getting Sterilized for Cash"; Jon Swaine, "Drug Addict Sterilized for Cash," *Telegraph*, October 19, 2010; Jane Beresford, "Should Drug Addicts Be Paid to Get Sterilized?" *BBC News Magazine*, February 8, 2010, http://news.bbc.co.uk/2/hi/uk_news/magazine/8500285.stm.
4. Deborah Orr, "Project Prevention Puts the Price of a Vasectomy—and for Forfeiting a Future—at £200," *Guardian*, October 21, 2010; Andrew M. Brown, "Paying Drug Addicts to be Sterilised Is Utterly Wrong," *Telegraph*, October 19, 2010; Michael Seamark, "The American Woman Who Wants to 'Bribe" UK Heroin Users with £200 to Have Vasectomies," *Daily Mail*, October 22, 2010; Anso Thom, "HIV Sterilisation Shock: Health Ministry Slams Contraception Idea," *Daily News* (South Africa), April 13, 2011; "Outrage over 'Cash for Contraception' Offer to HIV Positive Women," *Africa News*, May 12, 2011.
5. Adams, "Why Drug Addicts Are Getting Sterilized for Cash."
6. Gary S. Becker, *The Economic Approach to Human Behavior* (Chicago: University of Chicago Press, 1976), pp. 3–4.
7. Ibid., pp. 5–8.
8. Ibid., pp. 7–8.
9. Ibid., p. 10. Emphasis in original.
10. Ibid., pp. 12–13.
11. Amanda Ripley, "Should Kids Be Bribed to Do Well in School?" *Time*, April 19, 2010.
12. The results of Fryer's studies are summarized ibid. For the full results, see Roland G. Fryer, Jr., "Financial Incentives and Student Achievement: Evidence from Randomized Trials," *Quarterly Journal of Economics* 126 (November 2011): 1755–98, www.economics.harvard.edu/faculty/fryer/papers_fryer.
13. Fryer, "Financial Incentives and Student Achievement"; Jennifer Medina, "Next Question: Can Students Be Paid to Excel?" *New York Times*, March 5, 2008.
14. Fryer, "Financial Incentives and Student Achievement"; Bill Turque, "D.C. Students Respond to Cash Awards, Harvard Study Shows," *Washington Post*, April 10, 2010.
15. Fryer, "Financial Incentives and Student Achievement."
16. Ibid.
17. Ibid.
18. Michael S. Holstead, Terry E. Spradlin, Margaret E. McGillivray, and Nathan Burroughs, "The Impact of Advanced Placement Incentive Programs," Indiana University, Center for Evaluation & Education Policy, Education Policy Brief, vol. 8, Winter 2010; Scott J. Cech, "Tying Cash Awards to AP-Exam Scores Seen as

Paying Off," *Education Week*, January 16, 2008; C. Kirabo Jackson, "A Little Now for a Lot Later: A Look at a Texas Advanced Placement Incentive Program," *Journal of Human Resources* 45 (2010), http://works.bepress.com/c_kirabo_jackson/1/.

19. "Should the Best Teachers Get More Than an Apple?" *Governing Magazine*, August 2009; National Incentive-Pay Initiatives, National Center on Performance Incentives, Vanderbilt University, www.performanceincentives.org/news/detail.aspx?pageaction=ViewSinglePublic&LinkID=46&ModuleID=28&NEWSPID=1; Matthew G. Springer et al., "Teacher Pay for Performance," National Center on Performance Incentives, September 21, 2010, www.performanceincentives.org/news/detail.aspx?pageaction=ViewSinglePublic&LinkID=561&ModuleID=48&NEWSPID=1; Nick Anderson, "Study Undercuts Teacher Bonuses," *Washington Post*, September 22, 2010.
20. Sam Dillon, "Incentives for Advanced Work Let Pupils and Teachers Cash In," *New York Times*, October 3, 2011.
21. Jackson, "A Little Now for a Lot Later."
22. Ibid.
23. Pam Belluck, "For Forgetful, Cash Helps the Medicine Go Down," *New York Times*, June 13, 2010.
24. Ibid.; Theresa Marteau, Richard Ashcroft, and Adam Oliver, "Using Financial Incentives to Achieve Healthy Behavior," *British Medical Journal* 338 (April 25, 2009): 983–85; Libby Brooks, "A Nudge Too Far," *Guardian*, October 15, 2009; Michelle Roberts, "Psychiatric Jabs for Cash Tested," BBC News, October 6, 2010; Daniel Martin, "HMV Voucher Bribe for Teenage Girls to Have Cervical Jabs," *Daily Mail* (London), October 26, 2010.
25. Jordan Lite, "Money over Matter: Can Cash Incentives Keep People Healthy?" *Scientific American*, March 21, 2011; Kevin G. Volpp et al., "A Randomized, Controlled Trial of Financial Incentives for Smoking Cessation," *New England Journal of Medicine* 360 (February 12, 2009); Brendan Borrell, "The Fairness of Health Insurance Incentives," *Los Angeles Times*, January 3, 2011; Robert Langreth, "Healthy Bribes," *Forbes*, August 24, 2009; Julian Mincer, "Get Healthy or Else . . . ," *Wall Street Journal*, May 16, 2010.
26. www.nbc.com/the-biggest-loser.
27. K. G. Volpp et al., "Financial Incentive–Based Approaches for Weight Loss," *JAMA* 300 (December 10, 2008): 2631–37; Liz Hollis, "A Pound for a Pound," *Prospect*, August 2010.
28. Victoria Fletcher, "Disgust over NHS Bribes to Lose Weight and Cut Smoking," *Express* (London), September 27, 2010; Sarah-Kate Templeton, "Anger Over NHS Plan to Give Addicts iPods," *Sunday Times* (London), July 22, 2007; Tom Sutcliffe, "Should I Be Bribed to Stay Healthy?" *Independent* (London), September

28, 2010; "MP Raps NHS Diet-for-Cash Scheme," BBC News, January 15, 2009; Miriam Stoppard, "Why We Should Never Pay for People to Be Healthy!" *Mirror* (London), October 11, 2010.

29. Harald Schmidt, Kristin Voigt, and Daniel Wikler, "Carrots, Sticks, and Health Care Reform—Problems with Wellness Incentives," *New England Journal of Medicine* 362 (January 14, 2010); Harald Schmidt, "Wellness Incentives Are Key but May Unfairly Shift Healthcare Costs to Employees," *Los Angeles Times*, January 3, 2011; Julie Kosterlitz, "Better Get Fit—Or Else!" *National Journal*, September 26, 2009; Rebecca Vesely, "Wellness Incentives Under Fire," *Modern Healthcare*, November 16, 2009.
30. For a discussion of the bribery objection in relation to other objections, see Richard E. Ashcroft, "Personal Financial Incentives in Health Promotion: Where Do They Fit in an Ethic of Autonomy?" *Health Expectations* 14 (June 2011): 191–200.
31. V. Paul-Ebhohimhen and A. Avenell, "Systematic Review of the Use of Financial Incentives in Treatments for Obesity and Overweight," *Obesity Reviews* 9 (July 2008): 355–67; Lite, "Money over Matter"; Volpp, "A Randomized, Controlled Trial of Financial Incentives for Smoking Cessation"; Marteau, "Using Financial Incentives to Achieve Healthy Behaviour."
32. Gary S. Becker, "Why Not Let Immigrants Pay for Speedy Entry," in Gary S. Becker and Guity Nashat Becker, eds., *The Economics of Life* (New York: McGraw Hill, 1997), pp. 58–60, originally appeared in *BusinessWeek*, March 2, 1987; Gary S. Becker, "Sell the Right to Immigrate," Becker-Posner Blog, February 21, 2005, www.becker-posner-blog.com/2005/02/sell-the-right-to-immigrate-becker.html.
33. Julian L. Simon, "Auction the Right to Be an Immigrant," *New York Times*, January 28, 1986.
34. Sumathi Reddy and Joseph de Avila, "Program Gives Investors Chance at Visa," *Wall Street Journal*, June 7, 2011; Eliot Brown, "Help Fund a Project, and Get a Green Card," *Wall Street Journal*, February 2, 2011; Nick Timiraos, "Foreigners' Sweetener: Buy House, Get a Visa," *Wall Street Journal*, October 20, 2011.
35. Becker, "Sell the Right to Immigrate."
36. Peter H. Schuck, "Share the Refugees," *New York Times*, August 13, 1994; Peter H. Schuck, "Refugee Burden-Sharing: A Modest Proposal," *Yale Journal of International Law* 22 (1997): 243–97.
37. Uri Gneezy and Aldo Rustichini, "A Fine Is a Price," *Journal of Legal Studies* 29 (January 2000): 1–17.
38. Peter Ford, "Egalitarian Finland Most Competitive, Too," *Christian Science Monitor*, October 26, 2005; "Finn's Speed Fine Is a Bit Rich," BBC News, February 10, 2004, http://news.bbc.co.uk/2/hi/business/3472785.stm; "Nokia Boss Gets Re-

cord Speeding Fine," BBC News, January 14, 2002, http://news.bbc.co.uk/2/hi/europe/1759791.stm.

39. Sandra Chereb, "Pedal-to-Metal Will Fill Nevada Budget Woes?" Associated Press State and Local Wire, September 4, 2010; Rex Roy, "Pay to Speed in Nevada," AOL original, October 2, 2010, http://autos.aol.com/article/pay-to-speed-nevada/.
40. Henry Chu, "Paris Metro's Cheaters Say Solidarity Is the Ticket," *Los Angeles Times*, June 22, 2010.
41. Malcolm Moore, "China's One-Child Policy Undermined by the Rich," *Telegraph* (London), June 15, 2009; Michael Bristow, "Grey Areas in China's One-Child Policy," BBC News, September 21, 2007, http://news.bbc.co.uk/2/hi/asia-pacific/7002201.stm; Clifford Coonan, "China Eases Rules on One Child Policy," *Independent* (London), April 1, 2011; Zhang Ming'ai, "Heavy Fines for Violators of One-Child Policy," china.org.cn, September 18, 2007, www.china.org.cn/english/government/224913.htm.
42. "Beijing to Fine Celebrities Who Break 'One Child' Rule," Xinhua news agency, January 20, 2008, http://english.sina.com/china/1/2008/0120/142656.html; Melinda Liu, "China's One Child Left Behind," *Newsweek*, January 19, 2008; Moore, "China's One-Child Policy Undermined by the Rich."
43. Kenneth E. Boulding, *The Meaning of the Twentieth Century* (New York: Harper, 1964), pp. 135–36.
44. David de la Croix and Axel Gosseries, "Procreation, Migration and Tradable Quotas," CORE Discussion Paper No. 2006/98, November 2006, available at SSRN, http://ssrn.com/abstract=970294.
45. Michael J. Sandel, "It's Immoral to Buy the Right to Pollute," *New York Times*, December 15, 1997.
46. Letters to the editor by Sanford E. Gaines, Michael Leifman, Eric S. Maskin, Steven Shavell, Robert N. Stavins, "Emissions Trading Will Lead to Less Pollution," *New York Times*, December 17, 1997. Several of the letters, along with the original article, are reprinted in Robert N. Stavins, ed., *Economics of the Environment: Selected Readings*, 5th ed. (New York: Norton, 2005), pp. 355–58. See also Mark Sagoff, "Controlling Global Climate: The Debate over Pollution Trading," *Report from the Institute for Philosophy & Public Policy* 19, no. 1 (Winter 1999).
47. A word in my own defense. The original article didn't actually claim that emitting carbon dioxide is intrinsically objectionable, though the provocative headline, IT'S IMMORAL TO BUY THE RIGHT TO POLLUTE (the editor's choice, not mine), may have encouraged this interpretation. That many people read it that way is reason enough to clarify my objection. I am grateful to Peter Cannavo and Joshua Cohen for discussion of this point. I am also indebted to Jeffrey Skopek, then a Harvard Law School student, who wrote an illuminating paper for my seminar on this issue.
48. Paul Krugman, "Green Economics," *New York Times Magazine*, April 11, 2010.

49. See Richard B. Stewart, "Controlling Environmental Risks Through Economic Incentives," *Columbia Journal of Environmental Law* 13 (1988): 153–69; Bruce A. Ackerman and Richard B. Stewart, "Reforming Environmental Law," *Stanford Law Review* 37 (1985); Bruce A. Ackerman and Richard B. Stewart, "Reforming Environmental Law: The Democratic Case for Market Incentives," *Columbia Journal of Environmental Law* 13 (1988): 171–99; Lisa Heinzerling, "Selling Pollution, Forcing Democracy," *Stanford Environmental Law Journal* 14 (1995): 300–44. See generally Stavins, *Economics of the Environment.*
50. John M. Broder, "From a Theory to a Consensus on Emissions," *New York Times*, May 17, 2009; Krugman, "Green Economics."
51. Broder, "From a Theory to a Consensus on Emissions." For a critical appraisal of the cap-and-trade approach to sulfur emissions, see James Hansen, "Cap and Fade," *New York Times*, December 7, 2009.
52. See BP "target neutral" website, www.bp.com/sectionbodycopy.do?categoryId=9080&contentId=7058126; £20 yearly estimate is at www.bp.com/sectiongenericarticle.do?categoryId=9032616&contentId=7038962; for British Airways carbon offset projects, see www.britishairways.com/travel/csr-projects/public/en_gb.
53. Jeffrey M. Skopek, a student in my Harvard Law School seminar, elaborates this critique of carbon offsets effectively in "Note: Uncommon Goods: On Environmental Virtues and Voluntary Carbon Offsets," *Harvard Law Review* 123, no. 8 (June 2010): 2065–87.
54. For a defense of carbon offsets by a thoughtful economist, see Robert M. Frank, "Carbon Offsets: A Small Price to Pay for Efficiency," *New York Times*, May 31, 2009.
55. Brendan Borrell, "Saving the Rhino Through Sacrifice," *Bloomberg Businessweek*, December 9, 2010.
56. Ibid.
57. C. J. Chivers, "A Big Game," *New York Times Magazine*, August 25, 2002.
58. Ibid.
59. Paul A. Samuelson, *Economics: An Introductory Analysis*, 4th ed. (New York: McGraw-Hill, 1958), pp. 6–7.
60. N. Gregory Mankiw, *Principles of Economics*, 3rd ed. (Mason, OH: Thomson South-Western, 2004), p. 4.
61. Steven D. Levitt and Stephen J. Dubner, *Freakonomics: A Rogue Economist Explores the Hidden Side of Everything*, revised and expanded ed. (New York: William Morrow, 2006), p. 16.
62. For an illuminating discussion of the concept of incentives and its history, see Ruth W. Grant, "Ethics and Incentives: A Political Approach," *American Political Science Review* 100 (February 2006): 29–39.

63. Google Books Ngram Viewer, http://ngrams.googlelabs.com/graph?content=incentives&year_start=1940&year_end=2008&corpus=0&smoothing=3. Accessed September 9, 2011.
64. Levitt and Dubner, *Freakonomics*, p. 16.
65. Ibid., p. 17.
66. Google Books Ngram Viewer, http://ngrams.googlelabs.com/graph?content=incentivize&year_start=1990&year_end=2008&008corpus=0&smoothing=3. Accessed September 9, 2011.
67. LexisNexis academic search of major newspapers by decade for "incentivize" or "incentivise." Accessed September 9, 2011.
68. Data compiled from the American Presidency Project, University of California, Santa Barbara, archive of Public Papers of the Presidents,www.presidency.ucsb.edu/ws/index.php#1TLVOyrZt.
69. Prime minister's speech at the World Economic Forum, Davos, January 28, 2011, www.number10.gov.uk/news/prime-ministers-speech-at-the-world-economic-forum/; Cameron quoted following London riots in John F. Burns and Alan Cowell, "After Riots, British Leaders Offer Divergent Proposals," *New York Times*, August 16, 2011.
70. Levitt and Dubner, *Freakonomics*, pp. 190, 46, 11.
71. Mankiw, *Principles of Economics*, 3rd ed., p. 148.
72. For a fuller discussion of this objection to utilitarianism, see Michael J. Sandel, *Justice: What's the Right Thing to Do?* (New York: Farrar, Straus and Giroux, 2009), pp. 41–48, 52–56.

3. How Markets Crowd Out Morals

1. Daniel E. Slotnik, "Too Few Friends? A Web Site Lets You Buy Some (and They're Hot)," *New York Times*, February 26, 2007.
2. Heathcliff Rothman, "I'd Really Like to Thank My Pal at the Auction House," *New York Times*, February 12, 2006.
3. Richard A. Posner, "The Regulation of the Market in Adoptions," *Boston University Law Review* 67 (1987): 59–72; Elizabeth M. Landes and Richard A. Posner, "The Economics of the Baby Shortage," *Journal of Legal Studies* 7 (1978): 323–48.
4. Elisabeth Rosenthal. "For a Fee, This Chinese Firm Will Beg Pardon for Anyone," *New York Times*, January 3, 2001.
5. Rachel Emma Silverman, "Here's to My Friends, the Happy Couple, a Speech I Bought: Best Men of Few Words Get Them on the Internet to Toast Bride and Groom," *Wall Street Journal*, June 19, 2002; Eilene Zimmerman, "A Toast from Your Heart, Written by Someone Else," *Christian Science Monitor*, May 31, 2002.

6. www.theperfecttoast.com; www.instantweddingtoasts.com.
7. Joel Waldfogel, "The Deadweight Loss of Christmas," *American Economic Review* 83, no. 5 (December 1993): 1328–36; Joel Waldfogel, *Scroogenomics: Why You Shouldn't Buy Presents for the Holidays* (Princeton: Princeton University Press, 2009), p. 14.
8. Waldfogel, *Scroogenomics*, pp. 14–15.
9. Joel Waldfogel, "You Shouldn't Have: The Economic Argument for Never Giving Another Gift," *Slate*, December 8, 2009, www.slate.com/articles/business/the_dismal_science/2009/12/you_shouldnt_have.html.
10. Mankiw, *Principles of Economics*, 3rd ed., p. 483.
11. Alex Tabarrok, "Giving to My Wild Self," December 21, 2006, http://marginalrevolution.com/marginalrevolution/2006/12/giving_to_my_wi.html.
12. Waldfogel, *Scroogenomics*, p. 48.
13. Ibid., pp. 48–50, 55.
14. Stephen J. Dubner and Steven D. Levitt, "The Gift-Card Economy," *New York Times*, January 7, 2007.
15. Waldfogel, *Scroogenomics*, pp. 55–56.
16. Jennifer Steinhauer, "Harried Shoppers Turned to Gift Certificates," *New York Times*, January 4, 1997; Jennifer Pate Offenberg, "Markets: Gift Cards," *Journal of Economic Perspectives* 21, no. 2 (Spring 2007): 227–38; Yian Q. Mui, "Gift-Card Sales Rise After Falling for Two Years," *Washington Post*, December 27, 2010; 2010 National Retail Federation Holiday Consumer Spending Report, cited in "Gift Cards: Opportunities and Issues for Retailers," Grant Thornton LLP, 2011, p. 2, www.grantthornton.com/portal/site/gtcom/menuitem.91c078ed5c0ef4ca80cd8710033841ca/?vgnextoid=a047bfc210VgnVCM1000003a8314RCRD&vgnextfmt=default.
17. Judith Martin quoted in Tracie Rozhon, "The Weary Holiday Shopper Is Giving Plastic This Season," *New York Times*, December 9, 2002; Liz Pulliam Weston, "Gift Cards Are Not Gifts," MSN Money, http://articles.moneycentral.msn.com/SavingandDebt/FindDealsOnline/GiftCardsAreNotGifts.aspx.
18. "Secondary Gift Card Economy Sees Significant Growth in 2010," Marketwire, January 20, 2011, www.marketwire.com/press-release/secondary-gift-card-economy-sees-significant-growth-in-2010-1383451.htm; card values listed are prices offered on the Plastic Jungle website on October 21, 2011, www.plasticjungle.com.
19. Offenberg, "Markets: Gift Cards," p. 237.
20. Sabra Chartrand, "How to Send an Unwanted Present on Its Merry Way, Online and Untouched," *New York Times*, December 8, 2003; Wesley Morris, "Regifter's Delight: New Software Promises to Solve a Holiday Dilemma," *Boston Globe*, December 28, 2003.

21. See Daniel Golden, *The Price of Admission* (New York: Crown, 2006); Richard D. Kahlenberg, ed., *Affirmative Action for the Rich* (New York: Century Foundation Press, 2010).
22. See comments by Yale president Rick Levin, in Kathrin Lassila, "Why Yale Favors Its Own," *Yale Alumni Magazine*, November/December 2004, www.yalealumnimagazine.com/issues/2004_11/qa/html; and comments by Princeton president Shirley Tilghman, in John Hechinger, "The Tiger Roars: Under Tilghman, Princeton Adds Students, Battles Suits, Takes on the Eating Clubs," *Wall Street Journal*, July 17, 2006.
23. I presented a version of these two objections to commodification in my Tanner Lectures at Brasenose College, Oxford University in 1998. In this section, I offer a revised version of that account. See Michael J. Sandel, "What Money Can't Buy," in Grethe B. Peterson, ed., *The Tanner Lectures on Human Values*, vol. 21 (Salt Lake City: University of Utah Press, 2000), pp. 87–122.
24. Bruno S. Frey, Felix Oberholzer-Gee, Reiner Eichenberger, "The Old Lady Visits Your Backyard: A Tale of Morals and Markets," *Journal of Political Economy* 104, no. 6 (December 1996): 1297–1313; Bruno S. Frey and Felix Oberholzer-Gee, "The Cost of Price Incentives: An Empirical Analysis of Motivation Crowding-Out," *American Economic Review* 87, no. 4 (September 1997): 746–55. See also Bruno S. Frey, *Not Just for the Money: An Economic Theory of Personal Motivation* (Cheltenham, UK: Edward Elgar Publishing, 1997), pp. 67–78.
25. Frey, Oberholzer-Gee, and Eichenberger, "The Old Lady Visits Your Backyard," pp. 1300, 1307; Frey and Oberholzer-Gee, "The Cost of Price Incentives," p. 750. The amounts offered ranged from $2,175 to $8,700 per year for the life of the facility. Median monthly household income of respondents was $4,565. Howard Kunreuther and Doug Easterling, "The Role of Compensation in Siting Hazardous Facilities," *Journal of Policy Analysis and Management* 15, no. 4 (Autumn 1996): 606–608.
26. Frey, Oberholzer-Gee, and Eichenberger, "The Old Lady Visits Your Backyard," p. 1306.
27. Frey and Oberholzer-Gee, "The Cost of Price Incentives," p. 753.
28. Kunreuther and Easterling, "The Role of Compensation in Siting Hazardous Facilities," pp. 615–19; Frey, Oberholzer-Gee, and Eichenberger, "The Old Lady Visits Your Backyard," p. 1301. For an argument in favor of cash compensation, see Michael O'Hare, "'Not on *My* Block You Don't': Facility Siting and the Strategic Importance of Compensation," *Public Policy* 25, no. 4 (Fall 1977): 407–58.
29. Carol Mansfield, George L. Van Houtven, and Joel Huber, "Compensating for Public Harms: Why Public Goods Are Preferred to Money," *Land Economics* 78, no. 3 (August 2002): 368–89.

30. Uri Gneezy and Aldo Rustichini, "Pay Enough or Don't Pay at All," *Quarterly Journal of Economics* (August 2000): 798–99.
31. Ibid., pp. 799–803.
32. Ibid., pp. 802–807.
33. Uri Gneezy and Aldo Rustichini, "A Fine Is a Price," *Journal of Legal Studies* 29, no. 1 (January 2000): 1–17.
34. Fred Hirsch, *The Social Limits to Growth* (Cambridge, MA: Harvard University Press, 1976), pp. 87, 93, 92.
35. Dan Ariely, *Predictably Irrational*, rev. ed. (New York: Harper, 2010), pp. 75–102; James Heyman and Dan Ariely, "Effort for Payment," *Psychological Science* 15, no. 11 (2004): 787–93.
36. For an overview and analysis of 128 studies on the effects of extrinsic rewards on intrinsic motivations, see Edward L. Deci, Richard Koestner, and Richard M. Ryan, "A Meta-Analytic Review of Experiments Examining the Effects of Extrinsic Rewards on Intrinsic Motivation," *Psychological Bulletin* 125, no. 6 (1999): 627–68.
37. Bruno S. Frey and Reto Jegen, "Motivation Crowding Theory," *Journal of Economic Surveys* 15, no. 5 (2001): 590. See also Maarten C. W. Janssen and Ewa Mendys-Kamphorst, "The Price of a Price: On the Crowding Out and In of Social Norms," *Journal of Economic Behavior & Organization* 55 (2004): 377–95.
38. Richard M. Titmuss, *The Gift Relationship: From Human Blood to Social Policy* (New York: Pantheon, 1971), pp. 231–32.
39. Ibid., pp. 134–35, 277.
40. Ibid., pp. 223–24, 177.
41. Ibid., p. 224.
42. Ibid., pp. 255, 270–74, 277.
43. Kenneth J. Arrow, "Gifts and Exchanges," *Philosophy & Public Affairs* 1, no. 4 (Summer 1972): 343–62. For an insightful reply to Arrow, see Peter Singer, "Altruism and Commerce: A Defense of Titmuss Against Arrow," *Philosophy & Public Affairs* 2 (Spring 1973): 312–20.
44. Arrow, "Gifts and Exchanges," pp. 349–50.
45. Ibid., p. 351.
46. Ibid., pp. 354–55.
47. Sir Dennis H. Robertson, "What Does the Economist Economize?" Columbia University, May 1954, reprinted in Dennis H. Robertson, *Economic Commentaries* (Westport, CT: Greenwood Press, 1978 [1956]), p. 148.
48. Ibid.
49. Ibid., p. 154.
50. Aristotle, *Nicomachean Ethics*, translated by David Ross (New York: Oxford University Press, 1925), book II, chapter 1 [1103a, 1103b].

51. Jean-Jacques Rousseau, *The Social Contract*, trans. G.D.H. Cole, rev. ed. (New York: Knopf, 1993 [1762]), book III, chap. 15, pp. 239–40.
52. Lawrence H. Summers, "Economics and Moral Questions," Morning Prayers, Memorial Church, September 15, 2003, reprinted in *Harvard Magazine*, November–December 2003, www.harvard.edu/president/speeches/summers_2003/prayer.php.

4. *Markets in Life and Death*

1. Associated Press, "Woman Sues over Store's Insurance Policy," December 7, 2002; Sarah Schweitzer, "A Matter of Policy: Suit Hits Wal-Mart Role as Worker Life Insurance Beneficiary," *Boston Globe*, December 10, 2002.
2. Associated Press, "Woman Sues over Store's Insurance Policy."
3. Schweitzer, "A Matter of Policy."
4. Ibid.
5. Ellen E. Schultz and Theo Francis, "Valued Employees: Worker Dies, Firm Profits—Why?" *Wall Street Journal*, April 19, 2002.
6. Ibid.; Theo Francis and Ellen E. Schultz, "Why Secret Insurance on Employees Pays Off," *Wall Street Journal*, April 25, 2002.
7. Ellen E. Schultz and Theo Francis, "Why Are Workers in the Dark?" *Wall Street Journal*, April 24, 2002.
8. Theo Francis and Ellen E. Schultz, "Big Banks Quietly Pile Up 'Janitors Insurance,'" *Wall Street Journal*, May 2, 2002; Ellen E. Schulz and Theo Francis, "Death Benefit: How Corporations Built Finance Tool Out of Life Insurance," *Wall Street Journal*, December 30, 2002.
9. Schultz and Francis, "Valued Employees"; Schultz and Francis, "Death Benefit."
10. Schultz and Francis, "Death Benefit"; Ellen E. Schultz, "Banks Use Life Insurance to Fund Bonuses," *Wall Street Journal*, May 20, 2009.
11. Ellen E. Schultz and Theo Francis, "How Life Insurance Morphed Into a Corporate Finance Tool," *Wall Street Journal*, December 30, 2002.
12. Ibid.
13. Schultz and Francis, "Valued Employees."
14. Tax deductions related to corporate-owned life insurance cost taxpayers $1.9 billion per year in lost revenues, according to a 2003 federal budget estimate. See Theo Francis, "Workers' Lives: Best Tax Break?" *Wall Street Journal*, February 19, 2003.
15. In this section, I draw upon my article "You Bet Your Life," *New Republic*, September 7, 1998.
16. William Scott Page quoted in Helen Huntley, "Turning Profit, Helping the Dying," *St. Petersburg Times*, January 25, 1998.

17. David W. Dunlap, "AIDS Drugs Alter an Industry's Math: Recalculating Death-Benefit Deals," *New York Times*, July 30, 1996; Marcia Vickers, "For 'Death Futures,' the Playing Field Is Slippery," *New York Times*, April 27, 1997.
18. Stephen Rae, "AIDS: Still Waiting," *New York Times Magazine*, July 19, 1998.
19. William Kelley quoted in "Special Bulletin: Many Viatical Settlements Exempt from Federal Tax," Viatical Association of America, October 1997, cited in Sandel, "You Bet Your Life."
20. Molly Ivins, "Chisum Sees Profit in AIDS Deaths," *Austin American-Statesman*, March 16, 1994. See also Leigh Hop, "AIDS Sufferers Swap Insurance for Ready Cash," *Houston Post*, April 1, 1994.
21. Charles LeDuff, "Body Collector in Detroit Answers When Death Calls," *New York Times*, September 18, 2006.
22. John Powers, "End Game," *Boston Globe*, July 8, 1998; Mark Gollom, "Web 'Death Pools' Make a Killing," *Ottawa Citizen*, February 15, 1998; Marianne Costantinou, "Ghoul Pools Bet on Who Goes Next," *San Francisco Examiner*, February 22, 1998.
23. Victor Li, "Celebrity Death Pools Make a Killing," Columbia News Service, February 26, 2010, http://columbianewsservice.com/2010/02/celebrity-death-pools-make-a-killing/; http://stiffs.com/blog/rules/.
24. Laura Pedersen-Pietersen, "The Ghoul Pool: Morbid, Tasteless, and Popular," *New York Times*, June 7, 1998; Bill Ward, "Dead Pools: Dead Reckoning," *Minneapolis Star Tribune*, January 3, 2009. Updated celebrity lists are posted at http://stiffs.com/stats and www.ghoulpool.us/?page_id=571. Gollom, "Web 'Death Pools' Make a Killing"; Costantinou, "Ghoul Pools Bet on Who Goes Next."
25. Pedersen-Pietersen, "The Ghoul Pool."
26. www.deathbeeper.com/; Bakst quoted in Ward, "Dead Pools: Dead Reckoning."
27. Geoffrey Clark, *Betting on Lives: The Culture of Life Insurance in England, 1695–1775* (Manchester: Manchester University Press, 1999), pp. 3–10; Roy Kreitner, *Calculating Promises: The Emergence of Modern American Contract Doctrine* (Stanford: Stanford University Press, 2007), pp. 97–104; Lorraine J. Daston, "The Domestication of Risk: Mathematical Probability and Insurance 1650–1830," in Lorenz Kruger, Lorraine J. Daston, and Michael Heidelberger, eds., *The Probabilistic Revolution*, vol. 1 (Cambridge, MA: MIT Press, 1987), pp. 237–60.
28. Clark, *Betting on Lives*, pp. 3–10; Kreitner, *Calculating Promises*, pp. 97–104; Daston, "The Domestication of Risk"; Viviana A. Rotman Zelizer, *Morals & Markets: The Development of Life Insurance in the United States* (New York: Columbia University Press, 1979), pp. 38 (quoting the French jurist Emerignon), 33.
29. Clark, *Betting on Lives*, pp. 8–10, 13–27.
30. Kreitner, *Calculating Promises*, pp. 126–29.
31. Clark, *Betting on Lives*, pp. 44–53.

32. Ibid., p. 50; Zelizer, *Morals & Markets*, p. 69, citing John Francis, *Annals, Anecdotes, and Legends* (London: Longman, Brown, Green, and Longmans, 1853), p. 144.
33. Life Assurance Act of 1774, chap. 48 14 Geo 3, www.legislation.gov.uk/apgb/Geo3/14/48/introduction; Clark, *Betting on Lives*, pp. 9, 22, 34–35, 52–53.
34. Zelizer, *Morals & Markets*, pp. 30, 43. And see generally pp. 91–112, 119–47.
35. Ibid., p. 62.
36. Ibid., p. 108.
37. Ibid., p. 124.
38. Ibid., pp. 146–47.
39. Ibid., pp. 71–72; Kreitner, *Calculating Promises*, pp. 131–46.
40. *Grigsby v. Russell*, 222 U.S. 149 (1911), p. 154. See Kreitner, *Calculating Promises*, pp. 140–42.
41. *Grigsby v. Russell*, pp. 155–56.
42. Carl Hulse, "Pentagon Prepares a Futures Market on Terror Attacks," *New York Times*, July 29, 2003; Carl Hulse, "Swiftly, Plan for Terrorism Futures Market Slips into Dustbin of Ideas," *New York Times*, July 29, 2003.
43. Ken Guggenheim, "Senators Say Pentagon Plan Would Allow Betting on Terrorism, Assassination," Associated Press, July 28, 2003; Josh Meyer, "Trading on the Future of Terror: A Market System Would Help Pentagon Predict Turmoil," *Los Angeles Times*, July 29, 2003.
44. Bradley Graham and Vernon Loeb, "Pentagon Drops Bid for Futures Market," *Washington Post*, July 30, 2003; Hulse, "Swiftly, Plan for Terrorism Futures Market Slips into Dustbin of Ideas."
45. Guggenheim, "Senators Say Pentagon Plan Would Allow Betting on Terrorism, Assassination"; Meyer, "Trading on the Future of Terror"; Robert Schlesinger, "Plan Halted for a Futures Market on Terror," *Boston Globe*, July 30, 2003; Graham and Loeb, "Pentagon Drops Bid for Futures Market."
46. Hulse, "Pentagon Prepares a Futures Market on Terror Attacks."
47. Hal R. Varian, "A Market in Terrorism Indicators Was a Good Idea; It Just Got Bad Publicity," *New York Times*, July 31, 2003; Justin Wolfers and Eric Zitzewitz, "The Furor over 'Terrorism Futures,'" *Washington Post*, July 31, 2003.
48. Michael Schrage and Sam Savage, "If This Is Harebrained, Bet on the Hare," *Washington Post*, August 3, 2003; Noam Scheiber, "Futures Markets in Everything," *New York Times Magazine*, December 14, 2003, p. 117; Floyd Norris, "Betting on Terror: What Markets Can Reveal," *New York Times*, August 3, 2003; Mark Leibovich, "George Tenet's 'Slam-Dunk' into the History Books," *Washington Post*, June 4, 2004.
49. Schrage and Savage, "If This Is Harebrained." See also Kenneth Arrow et al., "The Promise of Prediction Markets," *Science* 320 (May 16, 2008): 877–78; Justin

Wolfers and Eric Zitzewitz, "Prediction Markets," *Journal of Economic Perspectives* 18 (Spring 2004): 107–26; Reuven Brenner, "A Safe Bet," *Wall Street Journal*, August 3, 2003.

50. On the limitations of prediction markets, see Joseph E. Stiglitz, "Terrorism: There's No Futures in It," *Los Angeles Times*, July 31, 2003. For a defense of them, see Adam Meirowitz and Joshua A. Tucker, "Learning from Terrorism Markets," *Perspectives on Politics* 2 (June 2004), and James Surowiecki, "Damn the Slam PAM Plan!" *Slate*, July 30, 2003, www.slate.com/articles/news_and_politics/hey_wait_a_minute/2003/07/damn_the_slam_pam_plan.html. For an overview, see Wolfers and Zitzewitz, "Prediction Markets."
51. Quote from Robin D. Hanson, an economist at George Mason University, in David Glenn, "Defending the 'Terrorism Futures' Market," *Chronicle of Higher Education*, August 15, 2003.
52. Liam Pleven and Rachel Emma Silverman, "Cashing In: An Insurance Man Builds a Lively Business in Death," *Wall Street Journal*, November 26, 2007.
53. Ibid.; www.coventry.com/about-coventry/index,asp.
54. www.coventry.com/life-settlement-overview/secondary-market.asp.
55. See Susan Lorde Martin, "Betting on the Lives of Strangers: Life Settlements, STOLI, and Securitization," *University of Pennsylvania Journal of Business Law* 13 (Fall 2010): 190. The number of lapsed life policies for 2008 was 38%, according to *ACLI Life Insurers Fact Book*, December 8, 2009, p. 69, cited in Martin.
56. Mark Maremont and Leslie Scism, "Odds Skew Against Investors in Bets on Strangers' Lives," *Wall Street Journal*, December 21, 2010.
57. Ibid.; Mark Maremont, "Texas Sues Life Partners," *Wall Street Journal*, July 30, 2011.
58. Maria Woehr, "'Death Bonds' Look for New Life," The Street, June 1, 2011, www.thestreet.com/story/11135581/1/death-bonds-look-for-new-life.html.
59. Charles Duhigg, "Late in Life, Finding a Bonanza in Life Insurance," *New York Times*, December 17, 2006.
60. Ibid.
61. Ibid.
62. Leslie Scism, "Insurers Sued Over Death Bets," *Wall Street Journal*, January 2, 2011; Leslie Scism, "Insurers, Investors Fight Over Death Bets," *Wall Street Journal*, July 9, 2011.
63. Pleven and Silverman, "Cashing In."
64. Ibid. Quotations are from home page of Institutional Life Markets Association website, www.lifemarketsassociation.org/.
65. Martin, "Betting on the Lives of Strangers," pp. 200–06.

66. Testimony of Doug Head, executive director, Life Insurance Settlement Association, at the Florida Office of Insurance Regulation Informational hearing, August 28, 2008, www.floir.com/siteDocuments/LifeInsSettlementAssoc.pdf.
67. Jenny Anderson, "Wall Street Pursues Profit in Bundles of Life Insurance," *New York Times*, September 6, 2009.
68. Ibid.
69. Ibid.
70. Leslie Scism, "AIG Tries to Sell Death-Bet Securities," *Wall Street Journal*, April 22, 2011.

5. Naming Rights

1. Killebrew's salary in 1969 is from Baseball Almanac, www.baseball-almanac.com/players/player.php?p=killeha01.
2. Tyler Kepner, "Twins Give Mauer 8-Year Extension for $184 Million," *New York Times*, March 21, 2010; http://espn.go.com/espn/thelife/salary/index?athleteID=5018022.
3. Twins 2012 ticket prices at http://minnesota.twins.mlb.com/min/ticketing/season-ticket_prices.jsp; Yankees 2012 ticket prices at http://newyork.yankees.mlb.com/nyy/ballpark/seating_pricing.jsp.
4. Rita Reif, "The Boys of Summer Play Ball Forever, for Collectors," *New York Times*, February 17, 1991.
5. Michael Madden, "They Deal in Greed," *Boston Globe*, April 26, 1986; Dan Shaughnessy, "A Card-Carrying Hater of These Types of Shows," *Boston Globe*, March 17, 1997; Steven Marantz, "The Write Stuff Isn't Cheap," *Boston Globe*, February 12, 1989.
6. E. M. Swift, "Back Off!" *Sports Illustrated*, August 13, 1990.
7. Sabra Chartrand, "When the Pen Is Truly Mighty," *New York Times*, July 14, 1995; Shaughnessy, "A Card-Carrying Hater of These Types of Shows."
8. Fred Kaplan, "A Grand-Slam Bid for McGwire Ball," *Boston Globe*, January 13, 1999; Ira Berkow, "From 'Eight Men Out' to EBay: Shoeless Joe's Bat," *New York Times*, July 25, 2001.
9. Daniel Kadlec, "Dropping the Ball," *Time*, February 8, 1999.
10. Rick Reilly, "What Price History?" *Sports Illustrated*, July 12, 1999; Kadlec, "Dropping the Ball."
11. Joe Garofoli, "Trial Over Bonds Ball Says It All—About Us," *San Francisco Chronicle*, November 18, 2002; Dean E. Murphy, "Solomonic Decree in Dispute Over Bonds Ball," *New York Times*, December 19, 2002; Ira Berkow, "73d Home Run Ball Sells for $450,000," *New York Times*, June 26, 2003.

12. John Branch, "Baseball Fights Fakery With an Army of Authenticators," *New York Times*, April 21, 2009.
13. Paul Sullivan, "From Honus to Derek, Memorabilia Is More Than Signed Bats," *New York Times*, July 15, 2011; Richard Sandomir, "Jeter's Milestone Hit Is Producing a Run on Merchandise," *New York Times*, July 13, 2011; Richard Sandomir, "After 3,000, Even Dirt Will Sell," *New York Times*, June 21, 2011.
14. www.peterose.com.
15. Alan Goldenbach, "Internet's Tangled Web of Sports Memorabilia," *Washington Post*, May 18, 2002; Dwight Chapin, "Bizarre Offers Have Limited Appeal," *San Francisco Chronicle*, May 22, 2002.
16. Richard Sandomir, "At (Your Name Here) Arena, Money Talks," *New York Times*, 2004; David Biderman, "The Stadium-Naming Game," *Wall Street Journal*, February 3, 2010.
17. Sandomir, "At (Your Name Here) Arena, Money Talks"; Rick Horrow and Karla Swatek, "Quirkiest Stadium Naming Rights Deals: What's in a Name?" *Bloomberg Businessweek*, September 10, 2010, http://images.businessweek.com/ss/09/10/1027_quirkiest_stadium_naming_rights_deals/1.htm; Evan Buxbaum, "Mets and the Citi: $400 Million for Stadium-Naming Rights Irks Some," CNN, April 13, 2009, http://articles.cnn.com/2009-04-13/us/mets.ballpark_1_citi-field-mets-home-stadium-naming?_s=PM:US.
18. Chris Woodyard, "Mercedes-Benz Buys Naming Rights to New Orleans' Superdome," *USA Today*, October 3, 2011; Brian Finkel, "MetLife Stadium's $400 Million Deal," *Bloomberg Businessweek*, August 22, 2011, http://images.businessweek.com/slideshows/20110822/nfl-stadiums-with-the-most-expensive-naming-rights/.
19. Sandomir, "At (Your Name Here) Arena, Money Talks," citing Dean Bonham, a sports marketing executive, on the number and value of naming rights deals.
20. Bruce Lowitt, "A Stadium by Any Other Name?" *St. Petersburg Times*, August 31, 1996; Alan Schwarz, "Ideas and Trends: Going, Going, Yawn: Why Baseball Is Homer Happy," *New York Times*, October 10, 1999.
21. "New York Life Adds Seven Teams to the Scoreboard of Major League Baseball Sponsorship Geared to 'Safe' Calls," New York Life press release, May 19, 2011, www.newyorklife.com/nyl/v/index.jsp?vgnextoid=c4fbd4d392e10310VgnVCM100000ac841cacRCRD.
22. Scott Boeck, "Bryce Harper's Minor League At-Bats Sponsored by Miss Utility," *USA Today*, March 16, 2011; Emma Span, "Ad Nauseum," Baseball Prospectus, March 29, 2011, www.baseballprospectus.com/article.php?articleid=13372.
23. Darren Rovell, "Baseball Scales Back Movie Promotion," ESPN.com, May 7, 2004, http://sports.espn.go.com/espn/sportsbusiness/news/story?id=1796765.

24. In this and the next few paragraphs, I draw on my article "Spoiled Sports," *New Republic*, May 25, 1998.
25. Tom Kenworthy, "Denver Sports Fans Fight to Save Stadium's Name," *USA Today*, October 27, 2000; Cindy Brovsky, "We'll Call It Mile High," *Denver Post*, August 8, 2001; David Kesmodel, "Invesco Ready to Reap Benefits: Along with P.R., Firm Gets Access to Broncos," *Rocky Mountain News*, August 14, 2001; Michael Janofsky, "Denver Newspapers Spar Over Stadium's Name," *New York Times*, August 23, 2001.
26. Jonathan S. Cohn, "Divided the Stands: How Skyboxes Brought Snob Appeal to Sports," *Washington Monthly*, December 1991; Frank Deford, "Seasons of Discontent," *Newsweek*, December 29, 1997; Robert Bryce, "Separation Anxiety," *Austin Chronicle*, October 4, 1996.
27. Richard Schmalbeck and Jay Soled, "Throw Out Skybox Tax Subsidies," *New York Times*, April 5, 2010; Russell Adams, "So Long to the Suite Life," *Wall Street Journal*, February 17, 2007.
28. Robert Bryce, "College Skyboxes Curb Elbow-to-Elbow Democracy," *New York Times*, September 23, 1996; Joe Nocera, "Skybox U.," *New York Times*, October 28, 2007; Daniel Golden, "Tax Breaks for Skyboxes," *Wall Street Journal*, December 27, 2006.
29. John U. Bacon, "Building—and Building on—Michigan Stadium," *Michigan Today*, September 8, 2010, http://michigantoday.umich.edu/story.php?id=7865; Nocera, "Skybox U."
30. www.savethebighouse.com/index.html.
31. "Michigan Stadium Suite and Seats Sell Slowly, Steadily in Sagging Economy," Associated Press, February 12, 2010, www.annarbor.com/sports/um-football/michigan-stadium-suite-and-seats-sell-slowly-steadily-in-sagging-economy/.
32. Adam Sternbergh, "Billy Beane of 'Moneyball' Has Given Up on His Own Hollywood Ending," *New York Times Magazine*, September 21, 2011.
33. Ibid.; Allen Barra, "The 'Moneyball' Myth," *Wall Street Journal*, September 22, 2011.
34. President Lawrence H. Summers, "Fourth Annual Marshall J. Seidman Lecture on Health Policy," Boston, April 27, 2004, www.harvard.edu/president/speeches/summers_2004/seidman.php.
35. Jahn K. Hakes and Raymond D. Sauer, "An Economic Evaluation of the Moneyball Hypothesis," *Journal of Economic Perspectives* 20 (Summer 2006): 173–85; Tyler Cowen and Kevin Grier, "The Economics of *Moneyball*," *Grantland*, December 7, 2011, www.grantland.com/story/_/id/7328539/the-economics-moneyball.
36. Cowen and Grier, "The Economics of *Moneyball*."

37. Richard Tomkins, "Advertising Takes Off," *Financial Times*, July 20, 2000; Carol Marie Cropper, "Fruit to Walls to Floor, Ads Are on the March," *New York Times*, February 26, 1998; David S. Joachim, "For CBS's Fall Lineup, Check Inside Your Refrigerator," *New York Times*, July 17, 2006.
38. Steven Wilmsen, "Ads Galore Now Playing at a Screen Near You," *Boston Globe*, March 28, 2000; John Holusha, "Internet News Screens: A New Haven for Elevator Eyes," *New York Times*, June 14, 2000; Caroline E. Mayer, "Ads Infinitum: Restrooms, ATMs, Even Fruit Become Sites for Commercial Messages," *Washington Post*, February 5, 2000.
39. Lisa Sanders, "More Marketers Have to Go to the Bathroom," *Advertising Age*, September 20, 2004; "Restroom Advertising Companies Host Annual Conference in Vegas," press release, October 19, 2011, http://indooradvertising.org/pressroom.shtml.
40. David D. Kirkpatrick, "Words From Our Sponsor: A Jeweler Commissions a Novel," *New York Times*, September 3, 2001; Martin Arnold, "Placed Products, and Their Cost," *New York Times*, September 13, 2001.
41. Kirkpatrick, "Words From Our Sponsor"; Arnold, "Placed Products, and Their Cost."
42. A recent example of an electronic book containing product placement is described in Erica Orden, "This Book Brought to You by . . . ," *Wall Street Journal*, April 26, 2011; Stu Woo, "Cheaper Kindle in Works, But It Comes With Ads," *Wall Street Journal*, April 12, 2011. In January 2012, the Kindle Touch sold for $99 "with special offers" and $139 "without special offers," www.amazon.com/gp/product/B005890G8Y/ref=famstripe_kt.
43. Eric Pfanner, "At 30,000 Feet, Finding a Captive Audience for Advertising," *New York Times*, August 27, 2007; Gary Stoller, "Ads Add Up for Airlines, but Some Fliers Say It's Too Much," *USA Today*, October 19, 2011.
44. Andrew Adam Newman, "Your Ad Here on My S.U.V., and You'll Pay?" *New York Times*, August 27, 2007; www.myfreecar.com/.
45. Allison Linn, "A Colorful Way to Avoid Foreclosure," MSNBC, April 7, 2001, http://lifeinc/today/msnbc/msn.com/_news/2011/04/07/6420648-a-colorful-way-to-avoid-foreclosure; Seth Fiegerman, "The New Product Placement," The Street, May 28, 2011, www.thestreet.com/story/11136217/1/the-new-product-placement.html?cm_ven=GOOGLEN. The company has since changed its name to Godialing: www.godialing.com/paintmyhouse.php.
46. Steve Rubenstein, "$5.8 Million Tattoo: Sanchez Family Counts the Cost of Lunch Offer," *San Francisco Chronicle*, April 14, 1999.
47. Erin White, "In-Your-Face Marketing: Ad Agency Rents Foreheads," *Wall Street Journal*, February 11, 2003.

48. Andrew Adam Newman, "The Body as Billboard: Your Ad Here," *New York Times*, February 18, 2009.
49. Aaron Falk, "Mom Sells Face Space for Tattoo Advertisement," *Deseret Morning News*, June 30, 2005.
50. News release from Ralph Nader's Commercial Alert: "Nader Starts Group to Oppose the Excesses of Marketing, Advertising and Commercialism," September 8, 1998, www.commercialalert.org/issues/culture/ad-creep/nader-starts-group-to-oppose-the-excesses-of-marketing-advertising-and-commercialism; Micah M. White, "Toxic Culture: A Unified Theory of Mental Pollution," *Adbusters* #96, June 20, 2011, www.adbusters.org/magazine/96/unified-theory-mental-pollution.html; shopper quoted in Cropper, "Fruit to Walls to Floor, Ads Are on the March"; advertising executive quoted in Skip Wollenberg, "Ads Turn Up in Beach Sand, Cash Machines, Bathrooms," Associated Press, May 25, 1999. See generally *Adbusters* magazine, www.adbusters.org/magazine; Kalle Lasn, *Culture Jam: The Uncooling of America* (New York: Morrow, 1999); and Naomi Klein, *No Logo: Taking Aim at the Brand Bullies* (New York: Picador, 2000).
51. Walter Lippmann, *Drift and Mastery: An Attempt to Diagnose the Current Unrest* (New York: Mitchell Kennerley, 1914), p. 68.
52. For an account of the barns, along with some striking photos, see William G. Simmonds, *Advertising Barns: Vanishing American Landmarks* (St. Paul, MN: MBI Publishing, 2004).
53. Janet Kornblum, "A Brand-New Name for Daddy's Little eBaby," *USA Today*, July 26, 2001; Don Oldenburg, "Ringing Up Baby: Companies Yawned at Child Naming Rights, but Was It an Idea Ahead of Its Time?" *Washington Post*, September 11, 2001.
54. Joe Sharkey, "Beach-Blanket Babel," *New York Times*, July 5, 1998; Wollenberg, "Ads Turn Up in Beach Sand, Cash Machines, Bathrooms."
55. David Parrish, "Orange County Beaches Might Be Ad Vehicle for Chevy," *Orange County Register*, July 16, 1998; "Shelby Grad, "This Beach Is Being Brought to You by . . . ," *Los Angeles Times*, July 22, 1998; Harry Hurt III, "Parks Brought to You by . . . ," *U.S. News & World Report*, August 11, 1997; Melanie Wells, "Advertisers Link Up with Cities," *USA Today*, May 28, 1997.
56. Verne G. Kopytoff, "Now, Brought to You by Coke (or Pepsi): Your City Hall," *New York Times*, November 29, 1999; Matt Schwartz, "Proposed Ad Deals Draw Critics," *Houston Chronicle*, January 26, 2002.
57. Terry Lefton, "Made in New York: A Nike Swoosh on the Great Lawn?" *Brandweek*, December 8, 2003; Gregory Solman, "Awarding Keys to the Newly Sponsored City: Private/Public Partnerships Have Come a Long Way," *Adweek*, September 22, 2003.

58. Carey Goldberg, "Bid to Sell Naming Rights Runs Off Track in Boston," *New York Times*, March 9, 2001; Michael M. Grynbaum, "M.T.A. Sells Naming Rights to Subway Station," *New York Times*, June 24, 2009; Robert Klara, "Cities for Sale," *Brandweek*, March 9, 2009.
59. Paul Nussbaum, "SEPTA Approves Changing Name of Pattison Station to AT&T," *Philadelphia Inquirer*, June 25, 2010.
60. Cynthia Roy, "Mass. Eyes Revenue in Park Names," *Boston Globe*, May 6, 2003; "On Wal-Mart Pond?" editorial, *Boston Globe*, May 15, 2003.
61. Ianthe Jeanne Dugan, "A Whole New Name Game," *Wall Street Journal*, December 6, 2010; Jennifer Rooney, "Government Solutions Group Helps Cash-Strapped State Parks Hook Up with Corporate Sponsor Dollars," *Advertising Age*, February 14, 2011; "Billboards and Parks Don't Mix," editorial, *Los Angeles Times*, December 3, 2011.
62. Fred Grimm, "New Florida State Motto: 'This Space Available,'" *Miami Herald*, October 1, 2011; Rooney, "Government Solutions Group Helps Cash-Strapped State Parks Hook Up with Corporate Sponsor Dollars."
63. Daniel B. Wood, "Your Ad Here: Cop Cars as the Next Billboards," *Christian Science Monitor*, October 3, 2002; Larry Copeland, "Cities Consider Ads on Police Cars," *USA Today*, October 30, 2002; Jeff Holtz, "To Serve and Persuade," *New York Times*, February 9, 2003.
64. Holtz, "To Serve and Persuade"; "Reject Police-Car Advertising," editorial, *Charleston (South Carolina) Post and Courier*, November 29, 2002; "A Creepy Commercialism," editorial, *Hartford Courant*, January 28, 2003.
65. "Reject Police-Car Advertising"; "A Creepy Commercialism"; "A Badge, a Gun—and a Great Deal on Vinyl Siding," editorial, *Roanoke (Virginia) Times & World News*, November 29, 2002; "To Protect and to Sell," editorial, *Toledo Blade*, November 6, 2002; Leonard Pitts, Jr., "Don't Let Cop Cars Become Billboards," *Baltimore Sun*, November 10, 2002.
66. Holtz, "To Serve and Persuade"; Wood, "Your Ad Here."
67. Helen Nowicka, "A Police Car Is on Its Way," *Independent* (London), September 8, 1996; Stewart Tendler, "Police Look to Private Firms for Sponsorship Cash," *Times* (London), January 6, 1997.
68. Kathleen Burge, "Ad Watch: Police Sponsors Put Littleton Cruiser on the Road," *Boston Globe*, February 14, 2006; Ben Dobbin, "Some Police Agencies Sold on Sponsorship Deals," *Boston Globe*, December 26, 2011.
69. Anthony Schoettle, "City's Sponsorship Plan Takes Wing with KFC," *Indianapolis Business Journal*, January 11, 2010.
70. Matthew Spina, "Advertising Company Putting Ads in County Jail," *Buffalo News*, March 27, 2011.

71. Ibid.
72. Michael J. Sandel, "Ad Nauseum," *New Republic*, September 1, 1997; Russ Baker, "Stealth TV," *American Prospect* 12 (February 12, 2001); William H. Honan, "Scholars Attack Public School TV Program," *New York Times*, January 22, 1997; "Captive Kids: A Report on Commercial Pressures on Kids at School," Consumers Union, 1997, www.consumersunion.org/other/captivekids/c1vcnn_chart.htm; Simon Dumenco, "Controversial Ad-Supported In-School News Network Might Be an Idea Whose Time Has Come and Gone," *Advertising Age*, July 16, 2007.
73. Quoted in Baker, "Stealth TV."
74. Jenny Anderson, "The Best School $75 Million Can Buy," *New York Times*, July 8, 2011; Dumenco, "Controversial Ad-Supported In-School News Network Might Be an Idea Whose Time Has Come and Gone"; Mya Frazier, "Channel One: New Owner, Old Issues," *Advertising Age*, November 26, 2007; "The End of the Line for Channel One News?" news release, Campaign for a Commercial-Free Childhood, August 30, 2011, www.commondreams.org/newswire/2011/08/30-0.
75. Deborah Stead, "Corporate Classrooms and Commercialism," *New York Times*, January 5, 1997; Kate Zernike, "Let's Make a Deal: Businesses Seek Classroom Access," *Boston Globe*, February 2, 1997; Sandel, "Ad Nauseum"; "Captive Kids," www.consumersunion.org/other/captivekids/evaluations.htm; Alex Molhar, *Giving Kids the Business: The Commercialization of American Schools* (Boulder, CO: Westview Press, 1996).
76. Tamar Lewin, "Coal Curriculum Called Unfit for 4th Graders," *New York Times*, May 11, 2011; Kevin Sieff, "Energy Industry Shapes Lessons in Public Schools," *Washington Post*, June 2, 2011; Tamar Lewin, "Children's Publisher Backing Off Its Corporate Ties," *New York Times*, July 31, 2011.
77. David Shenk, "The Pedagogy of Pasta Sauce," *Harper's*, September 1995; Stead, "Corporate Classrooms and Commercialism"; Sandel, "Ad Nauseum"; Molnar, *Giving Kids the Business.*
78. Juliet Schor, *Born to Buy: The Commercialized Child and the New Consumer Culture* (New York: Scribner, 2004), p. 21; Bruce Horovitz, "Six Strategies Marketers Use to Get Kids to Want Stuff *Bad*," *USA Today*, November 22, 2006, quoting James McNeal.
79. Bill Pennington, "Reading, Writing and Corporate Sponsorships," *New York Times*, October 18, 2004; Tamar Lewin, "In Public Schools, the Name Game as a Donor Lure," *New York Times*, January 26, 2006; Judy Keen, "Wisconsin Schools Find Corporate Sponsors," *USA Today*, July 28, 2006.
80. "District to Place Ad on Report Cards," KUSA-TV, Colorado, November 13, 2011, http://origin.9news.com/article/229521/222/District-to-place-ad-on-report-cards; Stuart Elliott, "Straight A's, With a Burger as a Prize," *New York Times*, December

6, 2007; Stuart Elliott, "McDonald's Ending Promotion on Jackets of Children's Report Cards," *New York Times*, January 18, 2008.

81. Catherine Rampell, "On School Buses, Ad Space for Rent," *New York Times*, April 15, 2011; Sandel, "Ad Nauseum"; Christina Hoag, "Schools Seek Extra Cash Through Campus Ads," Associated Press, September 19, 2010; Dan Hardy, "To Balance Budgets, Schools Allow Ads," *Philadelphia Inquirer*, October 16, 2011.
82. "Captive Kids," www.consumersunion.org/other/captivekids/evaluations.htm. In this and the following two paragraphs, I draw upon Sandel, "Ad Nauseum."
83. 4th Annual Kid Power Marketing Conference brochure, quoted in Zernike, "Let's Make a Deal."

Acknowledgments

The origins of this book go back a long way. From the time I was an undergraduate, I've been intrigued by the normative implications of economics. Since shortly after I began teaching at Harvard in 1980, I have explored this topic by teaching graduate and undergraduate courses on the relation of markets and morals. For many years, I've taught Ethics, Economics, and Law, a seminar at the Harvard Law School for law students and Ph.D. students in political theory, philosophy, economics, and history. That seminar covers most of the themes in this book, and I have learned a great deal from the many outstanding students who have taken it.

I've also had the benefit of co-teaching courses with Harvard colleagues on topics related to this book. In the spring of 2005, I co-taught an undergraduate course, Globalization and Its Critics, with Lawrence Summers. The course turned out to be a series of vigorous debates about the moral, political, and economic merits of free market doctrine as applied to globalization. We were joined for some sessions by my friend Thomas Friedman, who more often than not was on Larry's side of the argument. I am grateful to them, and to David Grewal, then a graduate student in political theory and now a rising star on the faculty of Yale Law School, who educated me in the history of economic thought and helped prepare me for intellectual combat with Larry and Tom. In the spring of 2008, I co-taught a graduate course, Ethics, Economics, and the Market, with Amartya Sen and Philippe van Parijs, a philosopher who was visiting Harvard from the Université catholique de Louvain. Despite our broadly similar political outlooks, our views of markets diverge considerably, and I benefited greatly from our discussions. Although we have not taught a course together, Richard Tuck and I have had many discussions of economics and political theory over the years, and I've always been enriched and illuminated by them.

The undergraduate course I teach on justice has also provided opportunities to explore the themes of this book. On several occasions, I've invited N. Gregory Mankiw, who teaches Harvard's introductory economics course, to join us for discussions of market reasoning and moral reasoning. I am grateful to Greg, whose presence highlighted, for the students and for me, the different ways that economists and political philosophers think about social, economic, and political questions. On a couple of occasions, my friend Richard Posner, a pioneer in applying economic reasoning to law, has joined me in the Justice course for debates about the moral limits of markets. Some years ago, Dick invited me to join him and Gary Becker for a session of their long-running rational choice seminar at the University of Chicago, ground zero for the economic approach to everything. It was, for me, a memorable opportunity to test my arguments before an audience whose faith in market thinking as the key to human behavior was greater than my own.

My first formulation of the argument that became this book was in the Tanner Lectures on Human Values at Brasenose College,

Oxford University, in 1998. A fellowship from the Carnegie Scholars Program of the Carnegie Corporation of New York in 2000–2002 provided indispensable support in the early stages of this project. I am deeply grateful to Vartan Gregorian, Patricia Rosenfield, and Heather McKay for their patience, kindness, and steadfast support. I am also indebted to the summer faculty workshop at Harvard Law School, where I was able to try out portions of this project on a stimulating group of faculty colleagues. In 2009, an invitation from BBC Radio 4 to deliver the Reith Lectures challenged me to translate my arguments about the moral limits of markets into terms accessible to a nonacademic audience. The overall theme of the lectures was "A New Citizenship," but two of the four dealt with markets and morals. I owe a debt of thanks to Mark Thompson, Mark Damazer, Mohit Bakaya, Gwyneth Williams, Sue Lawley, Sue Ellis, and Jim Frank, who made the experience a great pleasure.

In this, my second book with FSG, I am indebted once again to Jonathan Galassi and his wonderful team, including Eric Chinski, Jeff Seroy, Katie Freeman, Ryan Chapman, Debra Helfand, Karen Maine, Cynthia Merman, and, above all, my superb editor, Paul Elie. At a time when market pressures cast long shadows over the publishing business, the people at FSG view bookmaking as a calling, not a commodity. So does my literary agent, Esther Newberg. I am grateful to them all.

My deepest debts are to my family. At the dinner table and during family travels, my sons Adam and Aaron were always ready with astute, morally considered responses to whatever novel ethical dilemmas about markets I tried out on them. And always, we looked to Kiku to tell us who was right. I dedicate this book to her with love.

Index

A NOTE ABOUT THE AUTHOR

Michael J. Sandel is the Anne T. and Robert M. Bass Professor of Government at Harvard University. His book *Justice: What's the Right Thing to Do?* was an international bestseller. He has been a visiting professor at the Sorbonne, Paris; delivered the Tanner Lectures on Human Values at the University of Oxford; and was the 2009 BBC Reith Lecturer. His writings have been translated into eighteen languages, and his lectures on Justice (www.JusticeHarvard.org) have been viewed, online and on television, throughout the world. In 2010, *China Newsweek* named him "the most influential foreign figure of the year" in China.